W9-CBW-873

# Investigation of Substance Abuse in the Workplace

Peyton B. Schur
James F. Broder, C.P.P.

**Butterworth–Heinemann**
Boston London Singapore Sydney Toronto Wellington

iv

**Library of Congress Cataloging-in-Publication Data**

Schur, Peyton B.
  Investigation of substance abuse in the workplace / Peyton B. Schur and James F. Broder.
    p.    cm.
  ISBN 0-409-90121-0
  1. Labor discipline—Law and legislation—United States. 2. Drug testing—Law and legislation—United States. 3. Substance abuse—United States. 4. Labor discipline—United States. 5. Drug testing—United States. I. Broder, James F. II.  Title.
  KF3540.S38     1990
  344.73′012598—dc20
  [347.30412598]                                          89-48821
                                                              CIP

**British Library Cataloguing in Publication Data**

Schur, Peyton B.
  Investigation of substance abuse in the workplace.
  1. Great Britain. Personnel. Alcoholism & drug abuse I. Title
  II. Broder, James F.
  658.3′822

  ISBN 0-409-90121-0

Butterworth–Heinemann
80 Montvale Avenue
Stoneham, MA 02180

10 9 8 7 6 5 4 3 2 1

Printed in the United States of America

# Contents

**PART III  TOXICOLOGY**

# Acknowledgment

The authors gratefully acknowledge all those who graciously gave advice and support for this project. Although the following list is by no means complete, we have tried to include the most notable contributions.

We are truly indebted to Cynthia E. Maxwell and Robert M. Lieber of the San Francisco law firm of Littler, Mendelson, Fastiff & Tichy. Their contribution to chapter 4, "Legal Considerations," was invaluable. Without a doubt, the key to our success in solving clients' problems has been enhanced by the application of labor law issues (such as the risk of wrongful discharge litigation) to the investigative process in order to reduce costly risks. The Littler law firm's annual labor law seminars are one of the authors' best sources of continuing education on these issues.

Over the years, many law firms and management associations have studied our work and offered their counsel, which has served to build and validate the concepts outlined in this book. By far the greatest contributors have been Kenneth E. Ristau, Jr., Kenneth W. Anderson, Willard Z. Carr, Jr., William D. Claster, Dennis A. Gladwell, Peter D. Holbrook, and Nancy P. McClelland of Gibson, Dunn & Crutcher; Wesley J. Fastiff, George J. Tichy II, Garry G. Mathiason, Robert F. Millman, Randolph C. Roeder, Michael J. Hogan, Richard S. Falcone, George E. Chaffey, Allen W. Teagle, Ruth Benson, Larry Song, Gordon Letter, Alan Levins, and Floyd Palmer of Littler, Mendelson, Fastiff & Tichy; Harry R. Stang of Bryan, Cave, McPhetters & McRoberts; Richard J. Simmons, Steven D. Weinstein, and Stuart W. Rudnick of Musick, Peeler & Garrett; Robert J. Kane and Bruce D. May of Stradling, Yocca, Carlson & Rauth; James C. Roberts of Graham & James; Michael A. Hood and Nancy L. Abell of Paul, Hastings, Janofsky & Walker; J. Rod Betts, Robert W. Bell, David B. Geardes, and James K. Smith of Gray, Cary, Ames & Frye; Edward H. Franzen, James G. Johnson, Kyle Brown, Jim Bowles, and John Brandler of Hill, Farrer & Burrill; Joel E. Krischer of Latham & Watkins; Stephen P. Pepe of O'Melveny & Meyers; Michael T. McColloch of Whitman & Ransom; Gary Moss of Wyman, Bautzer, Kuchel & Silbert; Edwin V. Woodsome of Munger, Tolles & Olson; Del Fuller and Joseph Creason of Pillsbury, Madison & Sutro; Ronald J. Klepetar of Rexon, Freedman & Klepetar; George E. Preonas, Kenwood C. Yoeman, and Keith A. Hunsaker of Seyfarth, Shaw, Fairweather & Geraldson; and John Alley of Alley and Alley. Also deserving of mention are Barbara L. Crouch and Gilbert Jacobi of the Merchants & Manufacturers Association, and The Executive Committee's Peter Lakey.

Likewise, it is important to acknowledge our friend, colleague, and associate Dr. Raymond C. Kelly for writing chapter 10, "Drug Testing in the Workplace," which adds a valuable dimension to this book.

We would also like to give special recognition to all our past and present clients for giving us the privilege of addressing their problems of theft and substance abuse. The experiences we continue to gain by working in a variety of environments and jurisdictions (we have handled cases in eighteen states) allow us to continually fine-tune our program.

Peyton B. Schur would like to express his gratitude for the exceptional professional experiences he gained during his employment with the firms of Industrial Security Analysts in New York City, Intercept, Inc., in Hollywood, California, and Krout & Schneider, Inc., in Los Angeles. Alan Coppage, Laurence Leif, Edward Gelb, and Eddy McClain of these firms provided valuable guidance and advice on the techniques listed in this book and provided a forum for the discussion of new theories.

A special note of thanks is due to Donald J. Broder, the brother of author James F. Broder. Without his assistance this book would not have had its beginning. And last but not least, we thank our wonderful friend, partner, and advisor Laurence A. Rauch, without whose faith and support our current enterprise would not have grown and flourished.

# Preface

Substance abuse has become epidemic in our society. As a result, employers are aggressively looking for ways to both prevent and detect this problem in the workplace. At the same time, civil libertarians are battling to preserve the employee's rights to privacy and protection from entrapment, coercion, and the intentional infliction of emotional distress. Accordingly, employers and the investigators they may hire should be aware of existing statutes and case laws that protect the employee's rights.

Litigation, however, is not the only pitfall. Employee morale is also a serious concern. To fail to do a legally and morally sound investigation, to apply the detection methodology overzealously, will surely defeat the goal of any process designed to provide a safe, sane, and productive environment for employees and employers alike.

In this book, we cover these issues and describe some of our experiences in guiding clients through the minefield of dealing with substance abuse. We also discuss many lessons that were learned through the misfortunes of clients other than ours and by agencies other than ours. We hope the reader will benefit from our coverage of the salient points of how to properly conduct an investigation into malfeasance in the workplace, with a special emphasis on substance abuse.

Through our experience in conducting hundreds of investigations in the workplace, a common denominator has become apparent. Most employees who transgress against company rules do so as a result of conditions that management can prevent. These conditions are almost always related to two major variables: the type of employee the company hires and the environment into which it places its employees.

The type of employee a company hires is greatly affected by its ability to investigate an applicant's prior employment record. The environment into which a new employee is placed is affected by several factors. The first factor is how well-conceived and well-documented are the company's policies. Another is how well those policies are communicated to the employees, both in writing and orally. Often, oral communication of policies covers not only their content but also the reasons for their existence. Finally, the environment is affected by how well supervisors are able to foster compliance through good supervision. Employees need to know that the consequences of being caught violating a policy outweigh any financial or emotional reward that might be gained through that violation. In sum, the most basic management principles—those of proper screening, training, and supervising—are critical.

Ironically, the private investigation industry is fraught with poor screening, training, and supervision. This may be because the most talented investigators come from public agencies, where few investigators receive management training. Unfortunately, it is an axiom in our industry that the better the investigative capabilities of a person, the less likely he or she is to be a good manager of other investigators, primarily because of this lack of training in management principles. Accordingly, very few investigative agencies are in a position to help their clients prevent the same problem from occurring in their workplace. After a successful investigation, an agency's client is likely to request advice on how to keep the investigated problem from recurring. We hope those in our industry who have not been trained in management and labor relations principles will learn enough about these subjects through this book to determine whether they have the ability to give such advice. We firmly believe that if the staff of an investigative agency realizes that they are not adequately familiar with the principles of screening, training, and supervising, they will also be professional enough to realize that they have a limited ability to help their clients initiate all but the simplest aspects of a preventative program. When an investigation reveals that the problem of substance abuse has reached serious proportions in a client's workplace, most investigators realize that the best course of action is to refer the client to a labor relations specialist.

The reader who has become overwhelmed with the myriad "solutions" to the tragedy of substance abuse would do well to remember that there is no one solution for any manifestation of the problem. There are many different approaches, and when used in the proper combinations, they can make the difference between success and failure. It is not uncommon for employers to focus on one "solution" that is palatable to them and hope it will become their cure-all. But employers' circumstances and work environments can vary greatly, and one "solution" rarely succeeds by itself.

It is our desire to put some of these issues before the reader as food for thought. Of course, these issues are very complex; many of the issues addressed in this book could be, and in some cases are, the subject of an entire textbook. Nonetheless, if one investigative agency or client avoids one lawsuit or loss of license, develops one great investigator, or makes one workplace a safer and better environment, our efforts in writing this book will have proven to be worthwhile.

# Introduction

This book details a five-phase approach for the detection and prevention of substance abuse and other problems in the workplace. This process may be applied successfully in investigating many other forms of malfeasance as well. Before fully examining the process, however, we will describe what led to its development.

Industrial security in the United States was in its infancy toward the end of World War II. Many of the people who formed the fledgling security industry had left the military to fill an ever-increasing need in private industry—a need that became acute as it became evident that loss of assets was a growing problem. Soon, productivity also became an issue. Industrialists looked for people to detect employees who would perpetrate acts that were adverse to the main goal of their businesses: to make a profit. The vast number of trained military police and intelligence experts seemed a natural choice. Thus began the industrial security era, which was based—at least initially—on the premise of detection.

Management soon began to see the folly of simply detecting thieves, substance abusers, and malingerers. They began to realize that a good number of the employees who violated policies were simply employees who could not resist temptation. They also soon learned that managers were often responsible for the very temptations to which these employees succumbed. Managers began to ask their "security experts" if it wouldn't make more sense to prevent the problem than to detect it. And so began the trend toward loss prevention.

We analyzed the merits of both the school of detection and the school of prevention and found that neither was completely effective. One day, while giving a speech, one of us (Peyton Schur) was asked the question, "How can we rid ourselves of the cancer of drug abuse in the workplace?" The word *cancer* struck a nerve in Mr. Schur. He soon realized that there were similarities between doctors' approaches to treating cancer and his idea for combining the best of the schools of detection and prevention into a more effective program to assist our clients.

To understand the analogy between the approaches to drug abuse and cancer, consider the story of an individual with a family history of lung cancer. Throughout life, this person has done several things that are commonly known to increase the risk of cancer: smoked cigarettes, eaten foods known to contain carcinogens, and lived in an area where the air is laden with industrial smog and soot. With increasing age, this individual begins to have difficulty, and even pain, in breathing. In the back of his or her mind a warning bell goes off: it could be lung cancer. Yet the fear of learning that it is cancer prevents this person from seeing a doctor for years, until the pain becomes unbearable.

During the initial visit the doctor determines how the patient has lived and what he or she may have done to increase the risk of lung cancer. Biopsies and other tests show that the patient does have cancer. Exploratory surgery is recommended to document the malignancy and to determine whether the cancer has spread to other areas of the patient's body.

The malignancy is found to be limited to the lungs, and the patient is considered to have a fifty-fifty chance of survival. Treatment by radiation, chemotherapy, or surgery is recommended.

After a period of treatment and close monitoring, the cancer is officially declared to be in remission, and the treatment is ended. The patient has survived the treatment and is back to ground zero. The doctor recommends measures the patient can take to help prevent a recurrence.

As readers review the five-phase approach to dealing with substance abuse in the workplace (starting in chapter 5) they will notice that it has many similarities to the tried and proven process of treating cancer. Just as the doctor spends time with the patient in order to determine whether the patient has done things that may have contributed to the development of cancer, a good investigative firm should spend time with its clients to determine what a company may have done to increase the incidence of malfeasance in the workplace. When in their infancy, most companies are more concerned with business plans, research and development, product design, and marketing than with the issues of proper employee screening, training, and supervision. It does not take long before the negative impact of this lack of concern is manifested in the form of theft, absenteeism, work-related accidents, poor quality control, and poor profitability. When the bottom line becomes affected, these companies often turn to professional investigators for help.

Once it has been determined that a company has been lax in its management style, the process of separating the malignant problems from the benign begins. This "surgical" process takes the form of an investigation, whether it be an undercover investigation, surveillance, a background investigation, or an interview process that includes the procuring of statements from witnesses.

The investigation often consists of confrontational interviews with the most serious transgressors against company policy. This aspect of dealing with the problem has the greatest potential for disaster. Claims by plaintiff's attorneys of invasion of privacy, entrapment, coercion, and the intentional infliction of emotional distress can lead to litigation that may kill the "patient" even though the "cancer" itself has been discovered and removed.

The successful separation of the malignant and benign problems most often correlates with the effectiveness of the employer's process of administering discipline. It is important that this book's recommendations on how to disburse discipline be adhered to closely. It is equally important, however, that in an effort to administer discipline equitably, an employer not leave any of the malignancy to fester and grow at a later date.

Of course, just like a good doctor, a good investigator will either furnish or recommend consultants who can advise a company on how to improve its management style so as to create an environment in which the problem will be less likely to recur. Our overall theory is to combine the best of both the old school of detection and the new school of prevention. It is easy to see that you cannot prevent a problem if it already exists. It therefore makes sense to identify the problem, remove it without killing the "patient," and then initiate procedures that will create an environment in which prevention will be most effective.

Chapter 3 contains some case histories that illustrate the effectiveness of the aforementioned five-phase approach. Unfortunately, not all companies complete all five phases. Much like cancer patients who endure the struggle to reach remission, only to continue in their inveterate ways, many companies go through the struggle of detecting the problem of substance abuse and removing it from the workplace, only to rest on their laurels, hoping that their dismissal of employees who violated company policy will have a deterrent effect. They put little effort into addressing the management issues that may have played a much greater role in causing the problem than management would like to admit. We are sad to report that more than half our clients receive very low grades for their efforts to make the improvements in management issues that would help prevent the problem's recurrence.

The promising news is that the clients who understand that they played a role in the problem through mismanagement are the ones that realize the greatest return on their investment. This can sometimes be measured immediately (for example, when there is a large recovery of stolen property). Other benefits are somewhat more esoteric. Improvements in productivity and quality control and a reduction in worker compensation experience-modification ratios sometimes take a year or more to become evident.

# PART I

## The Problems Faced by Employers

# Chapter 1

# What Could Happen:
# A Horror Story

What follows is an example of a worst-case scenario that might occur if a company realized it had a substance abuse problem and contacted an investigative agency to solve that problem but made numerous mistakes along the way. After we tell you the story, we will explain "what is wrong with this picture." This exercise is not meant as a blanket indictment of the practices of investigative agencies or their clients; it is simply a means of pointing out the pitfalls of proceeding with an investigation of substance abuse in the workplace without a carefully conceived plan.

The Acme Manufacturing firm received an anonymous letter. The letter named four employees who sold drugs in the workplace and alleged that at least 25 percent of the work force regularly used drugs in violation of the company's drug policy. According to the letter, at least 10 percent of the employees were addicted to cocaine and methamphetamines, and some also smoked marijuana. As a result, productivity was down, work-related accidents were up, and theft was rampant. The anonymous writer claimed to be a recovering drug addict and stated that he or she would soon have to resign if the company did not solve the problem, as it would be impossible to stay "clean" in the current work environment.

Without the advice of the company's labor attorney, the president of the firm contacted the Pro Investigation agency and requested a meeting to discuss the problem. The president of Pro was a former narcotics officer in the local police department. He had opened his agency several years ago and had a good reputation throughout the law-enforcement community. He was a capable investigator and knew the district attorney's standards for successfully prosecuting a case of illegal drug activity.

At the meeting, the president of the investigative firm told the client of his background. The client showed the investigator the anonymous letter. The investigator advised that the best way to detect drug dealing in the workplace is to insert an undercover operative into the work force. To confirm Pro's ability to do the job properly, the client asked for references. The investigator supplied the names of references from the police department and the last successful case the agency had completed. At no time during the meeting were any other issues discussed except how to successfully file a criminal charge should the investigation identify any drug dealers. The meeting lasted approximately half an hour.

The president of Acme Manufacturing contacted the investigator's references, who all said the investigator knew what he was doing. One, the previous client of the investigative firm, stated that her investigation was conducted successfully and that three drug dealers had been caught at her facility. Impressed by what he heard, the president of Acme Manufacturing hired Pro Investigation to start an undercover operation, with the proviso that the agency place an operative into the work force within one week.

Pro Investigation was a "generalist" firm: it handled worker compensation investigations, background investigations, shoplifting, domestic and civil investigations, and undercover investigations. Rarely did Pro run more than one or two undercover operations at a time; consequently, it did not have a large staff of trained undercover operatives. At this point the agency was running only one undercover investigation, which was not scheduled to conclude for another couple of months. As a result, Pro decided to hire another undercover operative to start the Acme assignment. Pro ran an ad in a local newspaper and received twenty responses. Only two of the applicants had any undercover investigation experience, and only three others had investigative experience of any nature. The agency, not wanting to waste a lot of time screening and training applicants, hired the applicant who seemed to be the most experienced undercover operative.

With no time to do a background investigation or train the operative, Pro quickly set up a meeting with the client. Fearful the client might be nervous if it found out the agency had just hired this operative, the president of Pro instructed the operative not to disclose this fact to the client and, if asked, to be vague about the length of his relationship with the investigative firm.

The hired operative was a little more experienced than the other candidates who had applied, but only in that he had worked one month longer on one assignment. In that assignment he had made three drug buys, all of which he said were successfully prosecuted. The president of Pro Investigation intended to check the applicant's background, but he simply did not have time to do it prior to the meeting with the new client. He decided to do the background investigation at a later point and to train the operative once he was in place.

The president of Acme was impressed with the personality of the operative and told the agency he would like to place him on the assembly line. The client also told the president of Pro that the easiest way to get the operative in place would be for him (the client) to tell the manufacturing manager that the operative was a "friend of a friend" for whom he wanted to do a favor by getting the young man a job. The president of Pro accepted this pretext and agreed to place the operative the following day.

Since the president of Pro had another client meeting to attend, he instructed his new operative to report to work at the facility the following day, and told him he would teach him how to write reports some weekend in the near future. Unfortunately, this never occurred. The president of the agency also instructed the operative to come to the office once a week with his reports, which he was to write on a daily basis. The operative was also told to call the agency when anything "remarkable" occurred, and otherwise to just check in "every few days."

The operative was told he was an independent contractor and therefore not entitled to overtime pay, worker compensation, or disability insurance benefits. The operative was provided with no incentive to finish the case, such as a bonus. The client was not told how long the case would take or how much it would cost, nor did he ask for this information at the outset.

Approximately two weeks into the assignment, not much information of value had been gathered. The client began to pressure Pro to either produce information or end the case. The president of Pro tried to reason with the client, stating that it normally took more than two weeks to obtain the needed information. The client argued that if that was the case, he should have been advised of that fact before the case began. The investigator contacted his operative and told the operative that unless some dramatic information was produced in the very near future, the case would end and the operative would be out of a job. It was suggested to the operative that he do whatever was necessary to come up with the information, but no specific direction was offered on how he should proceed.

The operative decided to increase his inquiries to Acme Manufacturing employees concerning both drug-related activities, and thefts. This caused many of the culpable employees to become suspicious of him. Nonetheless, two employees agreed to help the operative steal products from the firm, and one employee offered to sell the operative cocaine after work. The operative, knowing that the client wanted documentation of malfeasance committed on company time and property, convinced the employee who was willing to sell the cocaine to do it on the premises during working hours. The operative never determined whether the employee had ever previously sold drugs at work.

The following day the operative bought half a gram of cocaine in the bathroom of the Acme facility. After work he immediately called the investigative agency and was instructed to bring the cocaine into the office, which he did. The president of Pro placed the purchased cocaine in his unlocked desk drawer to hold it as evidence. He then called his client with the "good news."

The client authorized Pro Investigation to continue for one more week to try and turn up further information. Several days later the operative arranged to have his agency film a major theft of Acme's merchandise, performed by himself and the two Acme employees who had agreed earlier to help him steal the property. As the three of them loaded the stolen material into a pickup truck, the operative injured his back lifting one of the heavy boxes.

Later, still in pain, the operative ran into the employee from whom he had purchased the cocaine and told that employee how he had hurt his back. The employee suggested that the operative use some of the cocaine he had bought, as it would help him keep his mind off the pain. The operative said he had already used up the cocaine, whereupon the employee suggested that the operative come out to the employee's car. At the car, the employee produced more cocaine from his glove compartment and encouraged the operative to use the cocaine right there to help alleviate the pain. The operative complied, thinking it would help to maintain his cover. He later explained to his supervisor that he was afraid the employee would suspect that he was an operative if he didn't use the cocaine. He also said he felt there was potential for physical harm if he did not play along.

The client, upon hearing this new information and learning about the extent of the theft, was unwilling to wait for additional investigative developments. He insisted that the investigation be brought to a close, reasoning that he would soon be bankrupt if such large-scale theft were to continue unchecked. The president of Pro convinced the client that the next step should be to bring in a team of interviewers to confront the culpable Acme employees. Little planning was done for this step because information had been obtained on only three employees. The president of Pro thought that three interviewers would be sufficient to confront the three employees.

The next day the interviewers arrived at the Acme plant, only to discover that there was just one office suitable for interviewing employees. Also, the cocaine-selling employee was not at work; it was the first day of his two-week vacation, and he was out of the state.

For the most part, the interviews of the remaining two culpable employees were uneventful. One of them, although reluctant to be truthful at first, gave the interviewers a complete admission. The second, a union employee, demanded to have an attorney or union representative with her at the time of interview. The interviewer did not concede to this demand and continued trying to obtain a confession for an hour after the request for representation was made. He finally concluded the interview without having obtained an admission.

After the interviews were finished, a search of the employee's lockers and desks was conducted, even though the company did not have a search policy and had not contacted a labor attorney for advice. The interviewers reasoned that the lockers and desks were company property and therefore subject to search. On the basis of the confessions and the available evidence, the employer fired both employees, again without legal advice concerning the issue of disparate treatment.

The employee who had gone on vacation out of state returned to work two weeks later with full knowledge of not only the issues of the investigation but also the techniques used by the interviewers. This employee was fully aware that there was little chance for his continued employment, as the other two had been fired. He therefore refused to talk or confess to either the employer or the investigation agency's interviewers. Acme fired him for ''failure to cooperate with the company's investigation.''

Later, the employer tried to prosecute the three fired workers on the basis of the information gathered during the investigation. The local police, with whom the president of Pro Investigation had once worked, told the client that elements of the crime (the corpus delicti) had not been adequately documented, separate from the employee's confessions, and that he would therefore not be able to file a case with the district attorney. Infuriated, the president of Acme contacted the state attorney general, who eventually sent investigators to review the case.

The state investigators subsequently determined that there were serious problems with the investigation. The most grievous was that the operative had been allowed to buy illegal drugs without authorization from the local police department. (Most states, including the one in this hypothetical situation, do not give private investigators special privileges to buy, obtain, or use illegal substances, even though they may be in the pursuit of a just cause.) It was also established that the operative's supervisor illegally possessed a controlled substance, which he stored in his unlocked desk. The state investigators contacted the Bureau of Consumer Affairs, the regulatory authority that licenses investigators in the state, and disclosed these facts. The administrator of the Bureau of Consumer Affairs pressed for further information and learned that the operative was not a full-time employee of the private investigation agency. She also determined that the undercover operative did not hold an individual private investigator's license and therefore concluded that the entire investigation was illegal.

The administrator contacted the state Industrial Welfare Commission and reported the Pro Investigation agency for paying unlicensed investigators as independent contractors. The state had strict rules concerning which classes of employees were and were not exempt from overtime. The commission determined that Pro was also in violation of the state's Industrial Welfare Act.

Meanwhile, the undercover investigator, who was now done with the case, was unemployed. When he attempted to file for unemployment insurance, the clerk at the unemployment office told him that he was not eligible. Through one of the secretaries at Pro with whom he was friendly, the operative learned that his former employer was under the scrutiny of the state for not paying him overtime as a regular employee. The operative returned to the unemployment office and, after explaining the situation to an official there, was granted a hearing. In that hearing it was determined that Pro should have hired the operative as a regular employee and therefore ruled in his favor, thus granting him full unemployment benefits. The state then imposed fines and back-pay penalties in its judgment against the investigation firm. These penalties were to be paid not only to the operative in question but also to all former so-called independent contractors who had ever worked for the firm. These penalties amounted to a sizable sum of money.

Upon receiving the favorable judgment from the Unemployment Appeals Board, the operative filed a worker compensation claim against Pro Investigation for the back injury he incurred while moving the stolen merchandise at Acme, as well as for psychological stress (a nebulous yet increasingly popular claim). The state Worker Compensation Board also awarded a judgment to the operative, launched its own investigation, and subsequently fined the investigation agency for not carrying worker compensation insurance for its "independent contractors," whom they also judged to actually be full-time employees.

News of these inquiries reached the local newspaper. One of the discharged employees from Acme Manufacturing had an uncle who was a plaintiff's attorney. Upon realizing that the operative had not been properly licensed, the attorney urged all three of the discharged employees to pursue a class-action lawsuit, theorizing that because the investigation was illegal, none of the information it had yielded would be admissible in court. They filed a multimillion-dollar wrongful discharge suit, which led to a large punitive damage award being entered against both Pro Investigation and Acme Manufacturing. Acme then sued Pro in an attempt to recoup its damages from the investigative agency's insurance policy against errors and omissions. The agency, however, carried no such policy, and when a judgment was awarded to Acme, Pro Investigation was forced into bankruptcy.

Unfortunately, the problems did not end there for Pro. The state police, who arrested the operative for illegally buying, possessing, and using a controlled substance, also arrested the president of the agency for possession of an illegal substance after a search of his desk revealed the cocaine stored there.

The state Department of Consumer Affairs suspended the agency's license. The three former Acme employees filed separate suits against the investigative agency for the intentional infliction of emotional distress. They made several tortious allegations, including invasion of privacy. Most of the allegations were unfounded, but the agency was unable to prove this because its interviewers had not properly taken written and oral statements from the three culpable employees. Such statements could have proved not only which rules the employees knowingly violated, with whom, and why, but also that nothing procedurally wrong was done by the interviewees to obtain the written and oral statements concerning malfeasance!

If all this was not bad enough, the truth was that the real problem at Acme Manufacturing was that about one-third of the work force was actually involved in serious problems of drug-related malfeasance, and only a small percentage of the culpable employees were identified during the botched investigation. The problem continued to fester, and Acme Manufacturing eventually went bankrupt due to continued litigation, poor productivity, poor quality control, poor customer service, absenteeism, work-related accidents, and continued theft.

A tremendous number of mistakes were made on the part of both the Pro Investigation firm and its client. Most of them will be addressed in this book. The following were among the most serious errors:

1.  The client did not thoroughly request and then check numerous references of the investigative agency.
2.  Before the case began, only criminal prosecution issues were discussed. Labor law and relations were ignored.
3   The planning issues, as well as time allotted, were deficient.
4.  The client put unrealistic time constraints on the agency. This forced the agency to neglect important screening and training standards.
5.  The agency's investigators were not given classroom or field training in report writing, labor law, criminal law, entrapment, or police liaison.
6.  The client was not told that the operative was a newly hired and relatively inexperienced employee of the agency.
7.  The easiest method of operative placement was chosen. Often covers that describe the operative as a friend or connection of an executive also can later stigmatize the operative as a ''conduit'' to management. This can increase the time it takes for operatives to gain workforce acceptance.
8.  The operative was given little-to-no formal training *before* the case commenced.
9.  The agency did not require the operative to maintain daily telephone contact with a case supervisor, to file written reports daily, or to meet weekly with a supervisor.
10. The agency had no system of obtaining written reports quickly and transcribing them for timely review by a supervisor.
11. The agency violated the rules of the State License Commission and the Labor Commission (and good management sense) by hiring the operative as an indepen-

dent contractor instead of as an employee. As a result, they also violated wage and hour laws and failed to provide worker compensation, disability, and unemployment insurance.

12. The agency did not instruct the client what to do, what not to do, and how long each stage of the investigation could be expected to take.
13. The agency encouraged the operative to accelerate the case in order to catch people and save the assignment. For the consequence of such an action, see the following point.
14. Through the operative, the agency entrapped employees of the client into theft and drug sales.
15. The agency failed to review the client's insurance policy for information on its bond policy for discovery (of theft), subrogation, and proof-of-loss limitations.
16. The agency failed to instruct the client how to establish ownership of property to provide proof of loss for insurance claims.
17. The agency violated the criminal code by failing to arrange "agent" status for the operative through the local police department to authorize his purchase and possession of illegal drugs.
18. The agency illegally sanctioned the use of a controlled substance by the undercover investigator.
19. The president of the agency stored a controlled substance in his desk instead of marking it as evidence and submitting it to the police.
20. There was not adequate planning for the interview process.
21. The agency interviewers were not trained to know the state and federal labor law issues.
22. The company did not have a search policy, and investigators violated company employees' reasonable expectations of privacy by searching their lockers.
23. Due to poor planning, the confrontations commenced before it was determined one employee was on vacation. By the time that employee returned, he had already had a chance to practice his alibi.
24. The interviewers violated the Weingarten Rights of an employee during an interview.
25. Discipline decisions were made without the advice of competent labor counsel.
26. There was no public relations plan if the investigation were to be covered by the media.
27. The client's problem was aggravated, not solved.

We are not aware of any agency or client that has actually made all the mistakes cited in this chapter. Neither are we aware of any agency or client that has suffered as badly as those in this story. Unfortunately, however, the problems set forth in our scenario are fairly common in the investigative industry. It is our hope that this book will assist investigators and clients to properly plan and structure investigations in order to minimize the possibility that any of these problems may occur.

# Chapter 2

# The Scope and Impact of Drug Abuse

Over the years we have read many statistics concerning a variety of problems that plague our society. We are really not sure how these statistics are compiled. Does the government send questionnaires to every employer in the country, asking them to send in data that would reflect what portion of their worker compensation claims were directly attributable to drug abuse in the workplace? How about what percentage of the theft they experience is directly attributable to people who use drugs? We cannot think of any better source for these statistics than employers, but how would the employers willing to provide such statistics be able to get them in the first place? All of this begs a major question: Are any of the statistical figures we read based on any significant facts?

We decided to address this question by studying a small group: approximately six thousand employees of firms that have been our clients in the past five years. These employees have all confessed to various transgressions against company policies, ranging from mildly significant to serious. The statistics derived from our analysis thus apply only to the workers who were the targets of investigation within the clients' facilities. For instance, in a company with a work force of three thousand, an investigation may have centered on only one-tenth of the entire population (in this example, three hundred employees).

Four percent of all the employees we interviewed in these investigations admitted to selling drugs on company time and property for the purpose of making a profit. Another 2 percent admitted that they were drug dealers in the legal sense but rationalized that morally they were not drug dealers, as they sold drugs not for the purpose of making money but as a social act. These individuals knew people who wanted to buy drugs and people who sold them. As a favor to both, they bought drugs from one employee, sold them to another, and delivered the money from the sale to the drug-dealing employee without making a profit. Finally, an additional 23 percent admitted to using drugs, being under the influence of drugs, or both while on company time or property. The data we have compiled in this unscientific study indicate that approximately 29 percent of the employees of the firms in which we have conducted investigations in the past five years have committed drug-policy violations.

## COSTS

Although no one knows precisely how pervasive drug use is on company time and property, it is clear that the problem is on the increase. Federal studies estimate that between 10 and 20 percent of all U.S. workers use dangerous drugs on the job. Other research indicates that people who take drugs regularly—about 25 percent of the U.S. population, according to some estimates—are likely to use drugs at work or to sometimes be under the influence of a substance when they arrive at the workplace.[1] Of course, the use of drugs before coming to work is tied to the issue of workers' rights to privacy regarding their off-duty activities. As one of our friends, a labor consultant, likes to say, "Unfortunately, an employee cannot park his bloodstream, like his car, at the threshold of your business."

### Worker Compensation

The costs of drug abuse on the job are staggering. The consequences range from accidents and injury to death. Studies at the Research Triangle Institute in North Carolina have shown that drug abusers are three times as likely as nonusers to injure themselves or someone else.[2] Since 1975 about fifty train accidents have been caused by drug- or alcohol-impaired workers. The National Transportation Safety Board attributed a fatal 1983 air accident to illegal drug use. The autopsy showed that the pilot of the ill-fated aircraft had been smoking marijuana, possibly while flying. The National Institute for Drug Abuse estimates that nearly two-thirds of the people now entering the work force have used illegal drugs, and 44 percent have taken them during the past year.

Even the space program has not been immune from the plague. Dr. Howard Frankel, who was medical director of Rockwell International's space-shuttle division from 1981 to 1983, says he treated employees who were hallucinating on the job, collapsing from cocaine overdoses, and using marijuana, PCP, heroin, and numerous other drugs while they worked. Frankel estimated that 20 to 25 percent of the workers at Rockwell's plant in Palmdale, California, were under the influence of drugs, including alcohol, while on the job.[3]

### Shrinkage (Fidelity)

When auditors and accountants cannot otherwise classify a firm's loss of assets, they usually categorize it as "shrinkage." Security professionals generally agree that shrinkage is the result of external theft, internal theft, or bookkeeping error.

Unfortunately, management often acts to control shrinkage only after it reaches

---

1. From "Battling the Enemy Within," *Time* (17 March 1986).
2. See note 1.
3. See note 1.

unacceptable levels. This conforms to Astor's Fourth Law of Loss Prevention: "Effective loss prevention is always preceded by extensive losses."[4]

There is a saying that is becoming more prevalent among security professionals: "Drug abuse and theft go hand in hand." Many employees end up stealing from their employers and coworkers to support their expensive illegal drug habits.

## Productivity and Quality Control

Drug-related errors and accidents can take a heavy financial toll on a company. According to Dr. Robert Wick, corporate medical director for a major airline, a computer operator who was high on marijuana once failed to load the company's computer with the tape that controlled the airline's reservations system. As a result the system was out of service for about eight hours, costing the company $19 million.[5]

When productivity is sacrificed on the altar of drug abuse, a natural consequence is product liability. This is especially evident in the high-tech industries. The role of the person who works on an assembly line where computer chips are manufactured is just as important as that of the engineer who designed the system. As we have learned through the media in recent years, many of the missile guidance and firing systems crucial to the defense capability of our nation have been found to be faulty because of production errors. Was drug abuse in the workplace the culprit?

## Absenteeism

More than any other ailment, alcoholism breeds absenteeism, high medical bills, and reduced work quality. North Carolina's Research Triangle Institute estimates that alcoholism cost the U.S. economy $117 billion in 1983, up 30 percent from 1980.[6] These shocking figures are probably on the conservative side. Richard Pelletier, Clinical Coordinator of the Merrit Peralta Institute at the Chemical Dependency Recovery Hospital in Oakland, California, says that "dealing with alcohol abuse and alcoholism in the workplace will always be a problem because the use of alcohol is not only legal but is culturally acceptable." Unfortunately, other drugs that are commonly abused may be becoming culturally acceptable in many parts of the United States—especially marijuana, cocaine, and methamphetamines.

## Litigation

The cost of litigation as a result of poorly managed or planned investigations has been rising. Litigators in California, one of the most litigious states in the country, have esti-

---

4. Saul D. Astor, *Loss Prevention: Controls and Concepts* (Stoneham, Mass.: Butterworth Publishers, 1982). Copyright 1982 by Security World.
5. See note 1.
6. See note 1.

mated that three-quarters of the wrongful discharge cases that went before a jury were won by the plaintiffs. In the United States as a whole, the average corporate punitive damage award is for nearly half a million dollars. Because punitive damages are meant to punish those upon whom they are levied, they are rarely covered by a company's insurance policy. The really bad news is that even companies that persevered and won the litigation still essentially lost, because in 25 percent of the jury trials the average cost of defense was approximately one hundred thousand dollars.

Because of constant changes in the laws affecting labor cases, we will not even consider taking on an assignment unless the client retains competent labor counsel. Investigators can keep up with the most significant changes in labor law by attending labor-law seminars, which are presented on an annual basis by some large law firms. Such seminars are not, however, a replacement for competent counsel; lawyers not only have far more expertise in interpreting the law but also tend to keep up with the changes, which could occur on a weekly basis throughout the year. (See chapter 4 for further discussion of labor attorneys.)

# Chapter 3

## Case Histories

It is important that a company trying to rectify its mismanagement problems be careful not to spend more time for the cure than they lose by having the "disease." Some returns on the investment in a proper investigation are immediate, such as theft recovery, but the benefits in areas such as quality control, productivity, and worker compensation often take time to become evident. Because most managers are far from clairvoyant in their ability to predict the return on such an investment, we offer the following case histories. They illustrate how solving acute problems in the workplace benefited four different companies. Above all, they underscore the importance of having good systems in place for measuring deficiencies in various areas, so that the costs of investigating and preventing problems from recurring will not outweigh the losses to be investigated.

### QUALITY CONTROL

The management of a major manufacturer of computer components believed there was a serious problem of drug abuse in their workplace. Complaints from customers regarding product quality had increased at an alarming rate. Sales had declined by 25 percent over each of the preceding three years. Theirs was a dramatic example of how customers will go elsewhere if the quality of a company's product gains a reputation for being unreliable. Of course, quality control departments within manufacturing facilities play a big and important role in ensuring that this does not happen.

An undercover investigation disclosed that the company did indeed have a drug problem that affected both the manufacturing and quality-control departments. Not only was the product inferior at the time of manufacture, but the effectiveness of the department charged with the responsibility of detecting defects was also impaired.

Numerous drugs buys were consummated during the investigation, and over one hundred incidents of on-premises drug use and working under the influence of drugs were documented in the undercover operative's reports. Seventy-two employees were eventually confronted and interviewed on the basis of information gained through the initial investigation of approximately fifteen employees.

At the end of each interview a labor consultant determined that drug abuse was not the only reason employees were not manufacturing or inspecting the product properly. Most of the employees in the quality control department stated that supervision was poor to nonexistent on most days.

Forty-three employees were fired as a result of the investigation. The director of manufacturing was replaced. The position of quality control manager was created and a nationwide search was conducted to find a first-rate candidate.

Two years later, the company's profits had risen from approximately seventy-five million to two hundred million dollars per year. Consumer complaints about quality were almost nonexistent. Profitability and employee morale were reported to be at an all-time high.

## WORKER COMPENSATION

A national paper-manufacturing firm believed that there was a serious drug problem in one of its Los Angeles mills, which produced cardboard containers. As in the preceding case, several drug buys were consummated during the course of the undercover investigation.

The president and secretary of the workers' union were also employees of the company. Both union officers got word that the investigators were conducting confrontational interviews and demanded that they be present during all interviews with employees.

The first step in dealing with this problem was to explain that under the National Labor Relations Board decision concerning Weingarten Rights, union employees are only entitled to representation if they ask for it, and no interviewed employee had exercised his or her Weingarten Rights. The union officials threatened to tell the employees on the work floor not to cooperate with the investigation unless a union representative was present.

In response, the investigator in charge explained a little-known National Labor Relations Board decision regarding a similar situation. A shop steward was fired for telling employees not to cooperate with an investigation. The supervising investigator suggested that before the union officers did something that might jeopardize their employment, they should check with their national representatives to verify the NLRB's decision in that case. The officers agreed. By the time they were able to validate the board's decision, however, the first series of interviews was over. Soon the second series was completed, and eleven employees had made sworn declarations, both written and oral, that they had committed serious violations of the company's drug policy.

When the union officers met with the investigators the second time, their stance was much less aggressive. They said they were not pleased that the investigation had proceeded without them but appeared to be resigned to the fact that they could sit in on interviews only when employees requested their presence. The supervising investigator, sensing that it would be best for the company and union to be on the same side of the drug abuse issue, offered to let the union officers sit in on the remaining interviews with two provisos. The first was that the union representatives would not interrupt the interview unless asked to. They would, however, be allowed to answer any question an employee might ask of them, as long as their responses addressed only that question. The second proviso was that if the employee asked the union representative whether he or she should tell the truth, the representative would advise the employee to be truthful. To the amazement of both the investigators and the paper mill's management, the union agreed to these conditions.

The interviews went smoothly, and the union officers abided by the agreement. In well over fifty interviews, only two employees asked any questions of the union representatives. The interviewers surmised that the employees thought that the union representatives would interject if anything was wrong. What the employees did not know was that the representatives had agreed not to interrupt. On the two occasions when employees asked if they should tell the truth, the union officials said yes. One hundred percent of the remaining employees interviewed signed written statements and made tape-recorded oral declarations.

Only one union arbitration resulted from this investigation. In addition, the union filed one complaint against the company with the Equal Employment Opportunity Commission, which ruled in favor of the company. Both of the union officers told management (off the record) that these actions were brought because the union feared that if it did not fight the weakest case management had, it would be sued by the employees concerned for failure to represent them. Both actions were based on the company's firing of two employees who had been implicated by drug abusers in the workplace of having sold drugs on company time and property, even though the investigators had found no corroborating information. The employees who had made declarations against the fired workers were subpoenaed, and all but one appeared at the arbitration. The written and oral declarations obtained during the investigation were entered into evidence. All the subpoenaed witnesses' testimony was supported by the declarations they had made during the confrontational interviews. Only one employee perjured himself during his testimony. The firings were upheld by the arbitrator, partly because of the testimony but primarily because of the credibility of the written and oral declarations.

This case is a good example of how excessive worker compensation costs can justify the investment in an investigation. The annual premium of the plant's worker compensation insurance policy was approximately two million dollars. Within one year of the completion of the investigation, a careful audit revealed that the employees who were fired for serious violations of drug policy represented approximately one-quarter of the work force. This small segment of the work force, however, had been responsible for 60 percent of the worker's compensation claims filed in the previous two years for time lost because of accidents. The amount of money the plant saved in the first year alone was ten times the cost of the investigation.

## INTERNAL THEFT

Recently we were called to the heartland of America to conduct an internal theft investigation for a well-known computer manufacturer. Management had received anonymous tips that an organized internal theft ring was running a black market for their computers, but there were no substantive clues as to who was involved.

Two undercover investigators were placed in two different positions in two different facilities during the course of the investigation. As is often the case, little valuable information was gathered on the theft problem during the investigation. Several employees, however, were reported to have used illegal substances on company time and property, and the two investigators eventually made several drug buys on the premises during work hours.

This case involved one of the most intensive interview sessions we have conducted in our careers. By the end of the second day of interviews, it became evident to our team of five interviewers that the drug problem was substantial. Soon after, leads were developed concerning employees who had stolen computers. We obtained consent to search their homes, and the results were amazing. Some workers had filled entire garages with company products. As the interviews progressed, the list of employees involved in the theft of company property grew exponentially. Eventually we had eighteen interviewers working in three shifts for an average of twenty hours a day and a total of twenty days in a row. In the end, well over one hundred employees had been interviewed, and over three hundred had been named as serious violators of company policy. More than seventy-five employees were fired. The retail value of the computers and components recovered from the employees' homes and garages was over one and a half million dollars. This large theft recovery represented an immediate return on the cost of the investigation. Left unchecked, this problem would not only have continued but also would have probably grown. The company would have suffered continuing losses of untold proportions.

## PRODUCTIVITY

One of the largest plumbing-supply houses west of the Mississippi had a small distribution facility in southern California. The work force consisted of sixty-two warehouse employees. In examining the results of an inventory, company auditors noticed a dramatic increase in shrinkage. In addition, management had heard rumors concerning drug abuse.

An undercover investigation was initiated and quickly found that both drug abuse and theft were rampant in the facility. The undercover operative was able to infiltrate the theft conspiracy, witness drug use, and consummate drug buys on the premises. When the interview process was over, forty-four employees had admitted to both drug-related violations and theft. What made this case unusual was that all the employees implicated were guilty of both transgressions.

The company chose to fire all these employees after the investigation was brought to a close. In a follow-up call approximately ten months later, the president told us he had not replaced any of them; he was running the warehouse with the remaining eighteen honest employees. When asked how business was, he said it was better than ever; in fact, productivity had actually doubled, even though the work force was only about a third of its former size.

Productivity may be one of the hardest areas in which to pinpoint potential loss figures, but as this case dramatically shows, having a work force that is only one-sixth as productive as possible can be costly too. One of the most rewarding returns on a company's investment in an investigation is increased productivity and improved employee morale.

# Chapter 4

# Legal Considerations

Robert M. Lieber
Cynthia E. Maxwell

Owing to the high cost of legal fees for the defense of lawsuits, the prevention of litigation has become paramount. Even defending against a frivolous lawsuit can be costly and time-consuming. The worst-case scenario, however, is that in which a company loses a costly lawsuit, pays out both damages for negligence and punitive damages, and then finds out that its insurance carrier has either increased its premiums, declined to renew the policy, or cancelled the coverage completely.

Accordingly, investigators should always be concerned about the consequences of an exposed investigation. The possibility that the company and the investigative agency might be targets of charges that are actionable in a civil court should never be discounted. Improper conduct on the part of the investigative agency will more than likely result in an allegation of emotional distress, violation of labor law, or invasion of privacy. It is relatively easy for an employee to allege that as a result of an investigation, he or she was the victim of an intrusion into their privacy. The fact that an alleged violation occurred on an employer's premises does not provide a defense against claims based on the right to privacy. There is much case law to substantiate this point.

An employee who was a subject of investigation might also allege that there was a public disclosure of private facts about him or her that was "offensive to a reasonable person." Generally, a disclosure by an investigator to a client regarding the actions or conduct of an employee is not considered a public disclosure if it was made in a confidential manner or otherwise handled discreetly.

Some courts have held that a "reasonable investigation" does not constitute an invasion of privacy. When an investigation is based upon a legitimate or lawful interest on the part of a client (such as illegal drug use on company time and property or the protection of company assets against known or suspected theft) and is conducted in a proper and legal manner, an allegation of invasion of privacy will generally not prevail. *Nader* v. *General Motors* 25 N.Y. 2d 560. 225 N.Y. 2d 765 (1970), however, set a precedent that an otherwise permissible investigative approach can become actionable

The authors of this chapter are attorneys with Littler, Mendelson, Fastiff, and Tichy.

if it is carried to extremes or used for otherwise impermissible purposes. Employers put themselves at an advantage when they use competent, experienced investigative agencies whose expertise can help avoid potentially serious problems in this area.

Exposed or compromised investigations sometimes lead to a new bargaining demand by a union or a hardening of a union's existing position. If disciplinary action is taken or attempted as the result of an exposed investigation, a union might file a grievance alleging that its contract was violated because the investigation was conducted in an improper manner. If the arbitrators decide that the investigation was a violation of "fair play," the employer will most likely receive an unfavorable ruling.

The wrongful discharge suit is the civil litigation to guard against most carefully when conducting investigations in the workplace. Since the awards and costs to defend against these suits can be substantial, great care should be exercised during investigative activities that could result in firings. The object is to design an investigation that minimizes exposure to civil litigation yet optimizes the chance of resolving the issues of concern.

## THE IMPORTANCE OF HIRING A LABOR ATTORNEY

We strongly recommend that all clients seek the advice of competent labor counsel before, during, and after any investigation of wrongdoing in the workplace. The variations in work environments and unions and the constant changes in labor laws dictate that a company should not risk its assets in any manner without sound advice from both legal advisors and loss-prevention experts. It should be borne in mind that in most states it is impossible to insure against punitive damages.

### Existing Laws Change

There is a constantly growing body of case law concerning employer-employee relations. It is incumbent upon all investigators to have a working knowledge of all laws, state and federal, criminal and civil, that relate to their activities. Otherwise they are likely to fall into the trap of ignoring pitfalls that may have serious consequences. The case of *National Labor Relations Board* v. *Weingarten* (1973) is a good example of this.

Weingarten, the employer, refused to allow a union representative to be present at an investigatory interview with an employee. The National Labor Relations Board (NLRB), citing the National Labor Relations Act, Section 8(a) (1), ruled in favor of the employee and the union. Weingarten appealed to the U.S. Fifth Circuit Court of Appeals (485 F2d 1135, 1973) and won a judgment that denied the NLRB's order ("there was no requirement for a union representative to be present").

In 1975 the case was appealed in the U.S. Supreme Court (*National Labor Relations Board* v. *J. Weingarten, Inc.*, 420 U.S. 251), which ruled that the employer's denial of an employee's request that her union representative be present at an investigatory interview that she reasonably believed might result in disciplinary action constituted an unfair labor practice.

## Laws Vary from State to State

It is not enough for investigators to be knowledgeable about federal labor law as it relates to investigations in the workplace. There is also a growing body of state laws, and some states are more liberal than others in the way they deal with labor issues. California, for example, has liberal state and local laws regarding drug testing. On January 1, 1986, a law went into effect in San Francisco banning most employers from requiring drug tests of their workers as a condition of employment. The ordinance was the first of its kind in the country.

California court decisions also limit drug testing. The first challenge of a random drug-testing policy to come to trial in California was *Luck* v. *Southern Pacific Transportation Co.* (1987). The case involved a computer operator (Luck) who was fired in July 1985 for refusing to participate in a random testing program imposed by the employer. The jury unanimously decided in favor of Luck on her claims of wrongful discharge and violation of public policy, breach of the implied covenant of good faith and fair dealing, and intentional infliction of emotional distress. They awarded her $485,000 in damages. Luck's attorney stressed that Luck's job had no direct public safety implications and that the company was wrong to order testing without some cause to believe that a substance abuse problem existed. The appeals court affirmed the jury verdict.

Employers in California are also required to reasonably accommodate employees who wish to voluntarily enter drug or alcohol rehabilitation programs. Generally, the employer must allow the workers time off to participate in such programs unless this imposes undue hardship.

These are only examples of some of the legal restrictions imposed on employers in California. Other state and federal governments also restrict employers and their agents. Accordingly, it is advisable to seek legal counsel at the outset of any investigation.

In the following pages we will cite some examples of how case law affects investigations. These examples are set forth to illustrate some of the common legal pitfalls of which the employer and the investigative agency should be aware. Of course, the information provided is not legal advice but is information designed to alert readers to legal issues.

## CAUSES OF ACTION

### Intentional Infliction of Emotional Distress

Damages for emotional distress have long been recoverable on behalf of plaintiffs who suffer physical injury as a result of tortious conduct. For example, a plaintiff who has suffered physical injury in the course of false imprisonment or battery could recover damages for emotional distress as well as for physical injury. In addition, if a defendant intentionally inflicted emotional distress, and if that emotional distress resulted in foreseeable physical injury, a cause of action could be stated even if the defendant did not intend to cause the physical injury.

Historically, a cause of action could not be stated in the absence of the defendant's intent to cause harm or in the absence of physical harm. The modern approach, however, recognizes independent causes of action for intentionally or negligently inflicted emotional distress, even without physical harm. A plaintiff is entitled to recover damages for severe emotional distress without any accompanying physical harm if the distress is caused by extreme and outrageous conduct. The extreme and outrageous character of the conduct may arise from an employer's or investigative agency's abusing its position of actual or apparent authority over an employee. Furthermore, the defendant's knowledge of the plaintiff's susceptibility to emotional distress may also give rise to extreme and outrageous conduct.

## False Imprisonment

False imprisonment is the unlawful violation of the personal liberty of another. In most cases, false imprisonment is a misdemeanor. If, however, the false imprisonment is accompanied by violence, menace, fraud, or deceit, it may be elevated to the status of a felony.

False imprisonment usually begins with the false or improper arrest of an individual, either by a police officer or a private citizen. Private investigators may be guilty of false imprisonment if they make an illegal arrest, regardless of the circumstances. An investigator who furnishes inaccurate or false information to a police officer who subsequently makes an arrest is generally no less liable for the arrest than the police officer.

Although a thread of common law governs the circumstances under which a private citizen of the United States may make an arrest, statutes concerning citizen's arrests vary from state to state. In our experience, investigators (with the possible exception of retail agents involved in shoplifting cases) seldom find it necessary to make spontaneous arrests.

Private investigators are at greatest risk of being charged with false imprisonment during confrontational interviews with accused persons. If an investigator uses, threatens to use, or creates the reasonable fear that he or she will use force to detain the person being interviewed, it may be a cause of action for false imprisonment.

We recommend that a written record of every interview be placed in the case file. Ideally, all statements should be signed by the person who made them and witnessed by someone other than the interviewer. Every signed statement should include the following: "This statement was given freely and voluntarily on my part. No threats or promises were made to me as an inducement for this statement. This statement is true and correct to the best of my knowledge and belief" (or words to this effect).

If the subject refuses to sign his or her statement, the investigator should read it back to the subject in the presence of a witness; the investigator should ask the subject to confirm orally that the statement was freely and voluntarily given and to explain why he or she will not sign the statement. The interviewer and witness should then sign and date the statement and note in writing the reason the subject gave for refusing to sign it.

When the investigator is able to obtain neither a signed statement nor a witnessed oral agreement that the interview process was free of threats or coercion, he or she should clearly and repeatedly make statements during the recording of the interview that the subject was free to leave at any time. If it appears that it will be difficult to prove the voluntary nature of an interview or interrogation, the best strategy is to terminate the interview on the spot rather than to continue and thus expose oneself to the charge of false imprisonment.

It is desirable but not absolutely necessary to have every subject sign his or her statement. An unsigned but witnessed statement is generally as admissible as a signed statement, and in some cases is even more believable to a judge and jury. This is not, however, the rule with oral declarations; these are discussed in chapter 7, which focuses on interviewing techniques.

## Illegal Search and Seizure

A peace officer must follow the Fourth Amendment of the U.S. Constitution and federal case law in gathering evidence to ensure that it will be admissible in a criminal trial. The exclusionary rule (*Mapp* v. *Ohio* [1961]) holds that competent, material, and relevant evidence that was illegally seized is not admissible in a criminal trial. Most states, however, do not apply the exclusionary rule to private, nondeputized officers. The private investigator or citizen should be more concerned about the possibility of civil or criminal action as a result of an illegal search, trespass, assault, battery, theft, or invasion of privacy. The exception is when private investigators act as agents of the police, who may make an arrest on the basis of evidence furnished by the private investigators. The exclusionary rule may then apply to the findings of the investigation.

In commercial and industrial settings, investigations often involve searches of employees' lockers and desks and inspections or searches of persons entering or leaving a facility. Such searches may usually be performed if the worker concerned has agreed—whether at the time of the search, in advance of employment, or as a condition of employment or continual employment—to consent to such searches.

Advance consent to a search can always be revoked at any time. If the search is of a desk or a locker belonging to the company, however, the investigator may ignore the revocation with little concern for potential liability if the employee does not have a reasonable expectation of privacy. In order to decrease the employee's privacy expectation, a company should provide notices to its employees that it retains the right to search lockers, desks, and other company property without the employees' consent or knowledge. These notices should be included in the employee handbook, distributed separately to each employee, and posted at the entrances to the facility and in the areas where company lockers are located. Employees' expectations of privacy in the workplace can be further minimized by periodically switching the lockers, desks, and company vehicles they use. However, if the investigator uses force to conduct a search of a person after that person has revoked consent, that use of force will probably be considered both a tort and a crime.

In a workplace where there is a union, the investigator should be mindful of the following when planning any search:

1. Is the company's rule on searches permitted under the contract?
2. Is the search policy reasonable?
3. Is it applied fairly?
4. Have the employees received sufficient notice of the search rule?
5. Has the discipline administered to employees found guilty of the alleged infraction(s) been just?

All of these factors may be subject to determination by an independent arbitrator, which would be separate from an employer's liability for criminal or tortious conduct.

## Invasion of Privacy

In the state of California the legislative body has added to its penal code the following statement on the invasion of privacy: "Advances in science and technology have led to the development of new devices and techniques for the purpose of eavesdropping upon private communications . . . the invasion of privacy resulting from the continual and increasing use of such devices and techniques has created a serious threat to the free exercise of personal liberties and cannot be tolerated in a free and civilized society."

Although the statutes subsequently enacted largely concerned wiretapping, other means of invasion, such as two-way mirrors in public bathrooms and trespass for the purpose of invading privacy, were also covered. The punishment for criminal invasion of privacy is a fine for three times the amount of the actual damages (if any) sustained by the plaintiff.

The 1970 case of *Nader* v. *General Motors* is a good example of how this issue relates to investigative activities. In that case, the court held that "the mere observation of the plaintiff in a public place does not amount to an invasion of privacy. But, under certain circumstances, surveillance may be so overzealous as to render it actionable."

In another case, *Galella* v. *Onassis* (1972), The U.S. District Court of New York stated that the plaintiff's surveillance, close-shadowing, and monitoring of the defendant were clearly overzealous and therefore actionable. Moreover, the plaintiff's corruption of doormen, romancing of the defendant's personal maid, deceptive intrusions into her children's schools, and return visits to restaurants and stores to inquire about her purchases were all exclusively for the "purpose of gathering information of a private and confidential nature" and were thus actionable. Judgment was for the defendant, Onassis, and the court held that the "plaintiff [had] no right to invade [the] defendant's right of privacy."

Dean Prosser, in his book *Law of Tort* (2d ed., Berkeley, CA: *Boalt Hall Law Review*, 1955, 637–39) and his article "Privacy" (*California Law Review* 48 [1960]: 389) states that four distinct torts affecting four different interests of a person are all classified as invasions but otherwise have almost nothing in common, except that each represents an interference with the right of the person "to be let alone."

1. Intrusion upon the plaintiff's seclusion, solitude, or private affairs.
2. Public disclosure of embarrassing facts about the plaintiff.

3. Publicity that places the plaintiff in a false light in the public eye.
4. Appropriation, for the defendant's advantage, of the plaintiff's name or likeness.

According to Prosser, the first three torts are primarily concerned with the protection of the plaintiff's mental interest and are only part of the larger problem of the protection of an individual's peace of mind against unreasonable disturbance.

## Defamation of Character

Since the Law of Libel Amendment Act of 1888, the courts of England have defined a defamatory statement as one that "tends to lower a person in the estimation of right-thinking members of society generally, or cause them to be shunned or avoided, or to expose them to hatred, contempt or ridicule, or to convey an imputation on them disparaging or injurious to them in their office, profession, calling, trade or business." This definition of defamation generally applies in the United States as well.

In a limited number of situations, it is not necessary for the person who alleges the wrong to prove actual damages; it is sufficient to prove that the defamatory statements were made. Truth, however, is an absolute defense for such statements. If one cannot establish truth or claim some privilege, absolute or qualified, then one may be required to pay damages. This is often the case when one makes accusations of crime, loathsome disease, unchastity in a woman, or conduct that would tend to discredit the person defamed in the exercise of his or her trade, business, or profession. In most other situations, the person defamed must establish that actual damage occurred. The damage is usually quantified in a dollar figure as the basis of the lawsuit brought by the plaintiff.

## Willful Torts

A tort, which may be either willful or unwillful in nature, is defined as a civil, as opposed to a criminal, wrong. A willful tort is one in which a person intends the consequences of his or her acts to injure another or intends to commit an act that will result in the injury of another. A deliberate false statement by an investigator about a person to his or her employer is an example of a willful tort. An invasion of privacy might be alleged against an investigator who unlawfully searched a person, inspected that person's property (e.g., the contents of an employee's locker), or eavesdropped on that person's private conversations electronically or otherwise. On the other hand, a person who strikes and injures a pedestrian while driving a vehicle in a careless manner may be guilty of negligence, which is not a willful tort. Some willful torts that are of interest and concern to private investigators are false imprisonment, invasion of privacy, defamation of character, fraud and misrepresentation, conversion of property, and battery and assault. Some of these torts may carry criminal penalties as well.

## Negligence

Everyone has a duty to use reasonable care and due diligence in order to prevent another person from being injured or suffering damage. Negligence does not require an intent to injure or cause damage. It is the absence of the intent to use reasonable care and to exercise due diligence that characterizes negligence as an actionable tort.

When a person commits an act so gross, wanton, or reckless that it indicates a total disregard for the consequences of that act, it may be viewed as an intentional wrong. Such conduct may incur a heavy liability, usually in the form of punitive or exemplary damages. Punitive damages are often awarded as a special deterrent to such wrongful conduct because it is regarded as more reprehensible than simple negligence.

## Collateral Estoppel

Collateral estoppel is a bar against the relitigation of an issue that was litigated in a prior proceeding and was a critical and necessary part of the earlier judgment. Accordingly, a judgment regarding the issue in the first action is binding upon the parties in later litigation in which the same issue arises.

## Discrimination

The federal government prohibits discrimination on the basis of race, color, sex, national origin, religion, and age. State and local laws are often even more protective. For example, California also prohibits discrimination on the basis of physical handicaps, cancer-related medical conditions, and marital status. Investigations of substance abuse in the workplace and employers' enforcement of substance-abuse policy must be conducted with care to avoid liability for discrimination. Investigators and employers must treat employees equally, regardless of race, color, or national origin, and must avoid any action that would have a disparate and negative impact on any protected group. The following checklist will help guard against discrimination claims:

1. Have the company's rules on substance abuse been consistently enforced?
2. Does the company investigate suspicious conduct without regard to race, color, sex, or national origin?
3. Does the company investigate evidence of cocaine use in the executive suite as well as marijuana use in the warehouse?
4. Does the company ignore policy violations in some departments (e.g., lunch-time drinking on the premises by management) yet strictly enforce company policy in others?
5. Has the company placed all its employees on notice of its substance-abuse policy and its intentions to strictly enforce that policy?
6. Is the severity of employee discipline consistent?
7. Is the company consistent in offering rehabilitation to employees with substance-abuse problems?

A company can avoid liability for discrimination by carefully drafting a substance-abuse policy and enforcing it consistently. Investigations should be conducted with an awareness that substance-abuse problems can exist throughout a company—among clerical workers, truck drivers, warehouse employees, and executives.

## INVESTIGATIVE ERRORS
## THAT MAY IMPEACH CREDIBILITY

### Unfair Labor Practices

Interfering with, restraining, or coercing employees engaged in the exercise of their right to engage in concerted activity (e.g., form, join, and assist unions) is a violation of the National Labor Relations Act. It is clear that a private investigator hired by a company to conduct an undercover investigation of theft or drug-related activities on company time and property is acting as an agent of the employer. Painstaking care must be used to avoid even the appearance of improper investigative activity. If it can be shown or even suggested that the real purpose of the undercover investigation is to interfere with, restrain, or coerce employees engaged in the exercise of protected activities, the union and the employees may have claims against both the employer and the investigative agency.

### Suggestions on How to Avoid Union Conflicts

Almost any undercover operation in the workplace has the potential to attract an allegation of unfair labor practice. Because such investigations are generally concerned with the violation of company rules, they usually involve the surveillance and investigation of persons and their activities on company property. Any legitimate investigative technique or method, if used for anti-union purposes, may result in a charge of interfering, restraining, or coercing. Therefore, the employer and investigator must always consider the labor-relations perspective on investigatory activities. During initial and ongoing training, all undercover operatives should be given the following general guidelines for conducting an investigation in a union environment:

1. Do not initiate an undercover investigation during a time of hostile or militant union activity. Let the situation cool down first if at all possible.
2. Operatives should be knowledgeable about unfair labor practices so that they will not include inappropriate information on union activities in their written reports, which are placed in the agency's permanent files and often forwarded to the employer.
3. The personal opinions of undercover operatives should never interfere with the performance of their duties and responsibilities to the agency or the employer. Operatives should refrain from making derogatory oral or written statements about unions, union officials, and collective-bargaining or organizing activities.

## Searches on Company Property

The Fourth Amendment to the U.S. Constitution, and parallel provisions in many state constitutions, proscribe unreasonable searches and seizures. Generally, the Fourth Amendment applies to government; however, it also applies to searches conducted by private companies or persons acting as agents of government. Agency is not established merely by informing the police of discovered evidence of criminal activity (this topic will be discussed further later). However, if a company conducts an investigation or search at the request of the police, it is acting as their agent, and the Fourth Amendment thus applies. In part, this means that the company needs a valid search warrant; a warrantless search of protected areas, even at the request of the police department, violates the employee's Fourth Amendment rights, and evidence obtained through such a search is not admissible in a criminal proceeding. In addition, the employee could bring an action for damages against the company for violating his or her constitutional rights.

The Fourth Amendment only protects areas in which an employee may maintain a reasonable expectation of privacy. This reasonable expectation of privacy was recently discussed by the U.S. Supreme Court in *O'Connor* v. *Ortega* (1987). In its decision, the Supreme Court held that a physician working for a state hospital had a reasonable expectation of privacy in at least his desk and file cabinets. The physician did not share his desk or file cabinets with any other employee, had occupied the office for seventeen years, and kept personal materials in his office, including personal correspondence and medical files and correspondence from private patients who were unconnected with the hospital. The files of the physician's subordinates were also kept in his office. The court noted "that there was no evidence that the [employer] had established any reasonable regulation or policy discouraging employees such as the physician from storing personal papers and effects in their desks or file cabinets." Because the physician had a reasonable expectation of privacy in his desk and file cabinets, the Supreme Court held that the search of these areas was lawful only if it was reasonable under all circumstances. The matter was remanded to the lower court for an evidentiary hearing on whether the search was reasonable—that is, whether it was justified at its inception and whether, as actually conducted, it was reasonably related in scope to the circumstances that justified its initiation.

Although the case of *O'Connor* v. *Ortega* arose in the context of the Fourth Amendment, it is also useful in understanding the tort of invasion of privacy. Whether someone's privacy has been unlawfully invaded depends on whether there is a reasonable expectation of privacy. Courts also consider whether their recognition of the privacy right will adversely affect other legitimate societal interests, such as an employer's interest in a healthy and productive work force and the integrity of its premises.

In light of the Fourth Amendment and the right of privacy, employers and investigative agencies should take the precautions outlined below.

### Searches of Company Property

The company should provide written notice to all employees that lockers, desks, company vehicles, and all other company property are not private and that the company retains the right to enter or search them at any time of day or night without the employees' consent or knowledge. The purpose of this notice, which should be both included in the employee handbook and distributed separately to each employee, is twofold: to minimize the employees' expectations of privacy and to establish consent to searches as a condition of employment. The notice might read as follows:

> Locks, desks, vehicles and [fill in additional property] are company property and must be maintained according to company regulations. They must be kept clean and are to be used only for work-related purposes. The company reserves the right to inspect its property to ensure compliance with its rules and regulations.

As noted earlier, employees' expectations of privacy can be further diminished by periodically switching the lockers, desks, and company vehicles they use. The employer should retain a key or combination for every lock used on company lockers, desks, briefcases, and vehicles. The company should own and supply all the locks to enhance the perception that these items are company property.

## Searches of Employees' Personal Property

If an employer or investigative agency desires to search employees' lunchboxes, toolboxes, purses, and/or clothing, the company must provide its employees with clear notice that such searches are a condition of employment, because searches of this type involve intrusion into individuals' privacy. The notice should be included in the employee handbook disseminated separately to each employee, pointed out to new employees at the time of hire, and posted prominently at every entrance to the facility. It might read as follows:

> The company reserves the right to search, without notice, any object brought onto company property. Additionally, if a supervisor has a reasonable suspicion that an employee has in his or her possession weapons or unlawful drugs or alcohol, or objects associated with the ingestion of illegal substances, the supervisor may subject the employee to a search of his or her clothing and/or possessions. An employee who refuses to submit to such a search will be subject to discipline, up to and including immediate discharge.

Even if a company has properly placed employees on notice of its right to search their personal property, a search should be performed only if the employee consents to it at the time. For example, if a supervisor has a reasonable suspicion that an employee is engaged in drug use and wishes to search the employee, the supervisor should explain the basis for the suspicion and request that the employee consent to a search. If the employee refuses, the supervisor should remind him or her that the company rules require consent to searches and that refusal to comply subjects the employee to disciplinary action. If the employee still refuses, then appropriate disciplinary action should be taken. At no time, however, should a supervisor grab the recalcitrant employee's lunchbox, briefcase, purse, or other personal property, or attempt to search the employee without his or her consent. Such unauthorized actions could result in liability for assault and battery as well as for invasion of privacy.

## Wrongful Discharge

The discharge of employees must be based on factual evidence of misconduct or unsuitability, not mere allegations. Collective bargaining agreements often stipulate that allegations of wrongful discharge be filed as union grievances, which may ultimately be settled by an independent arbitrator or an administrative labor law judge. The employment-at-will doctrine permits an employer to fire workers who do not have contracts for specific terms of employment "for good cause, for no cause, or even for cause morally wrong" (*Payne* v. *Western & A.R. Co.* [1884]). In the past, legislatures codified this doctrine, and statutes and courts strictly applied it, upholding the discharge of employees even in unfair situations. For example, in the case of *Hablas* v. *Armour & Co.* (1959), a court upheld the firing of an employee after forty-five years of satisfactory service, just before the employee was due to be vested to receive a pension.

Today, the employment-at-will doctrine has been substantially eroded by legislative action and judicial decision. The first limitations came in the form of exceptions in which legislatures identified special circumstances under which an employer could not fire a worker at will. These statutory exceptions have been expanded and supplemented by judicial exceptions to such an extent that some argue that at-will employment is no longer the rule because it has been swallowed up by all the exceptions. Courts now expect employers to fire employees only with good cause and to comply with a covenant of good faith and fair dealing.

When discharges are based on evidence gathered during an undercover investigation, all the activities of the investigation must be able to withstand scrutiny for fairness. The investigative agency's conduct and the behavior of its investigators may be thoroughly reviewed and must be shown to be reasonable under all circumstances in order to support the employer's firing of the workers in question. During such a review, it must be found that the incidents leading to the discharges involved serious employee misconduct, that those incidents did not involve entrapment (or even the possibility of entrapment) of the fired employees, and that the employees knew that their misconduct was a serious infraction of company rules.

## POTENTIAL VIOLATIONS OF CRIMINAL LAW

Private investigators and undercover operatives do not have a license to violate any criminal or civil law. Undercover operatives, often working without the benefit of direct supervision, must be trained and experienced in recognizing all the potential risks of exposure to litigation that they may face during investigations. They must know the limits of permissible action, and when difficulties arise they must exercise good judgment to avoid taking any action that might needlessly expose them or their agency to criminal or civil liability.

### Controlled Substance Laws

Most states require private investigators (and all other private citizens) to comply with the laws that govern the use, sale, and possession of controlled substances. At times, private investigators and other on-site security investigators get so involved in a work-place drug investigation that they convince themselves that because they are "on the side of right," they are justified in buying or using drugs to preserve their cover or to obtain additional evidence. But succumbing to this temptation surely compromises the professionalism of the case and exposes the investigators to the risk of criminal prosecution. In order for private investigators to buy or possess controlled substances, most state laws require that they be agents of duly sworn law-enforcement agencies. Although the definition of "agent" varies from state to state, it generally refers to any non-sworn investigator or private citizen who is under the direct control and super-vision of a sworn police officer. It is the duty of the police officer to oversee the inves-tigation and ensure that it is carried out in compliance with the laws governing the obtaining of evidence so the inevitable criminal prosecution is not jeopardized.

We are not aware of any situation in which a law-enforcement agency would justify the use of drugs by an undercover investigator to maintain his or her cover. The only possible reason an investigator might need to use drugs during an investigation would be to preserve his or her personal safety. However, the situation is extremely rare. Nonetheless, guidelines against drug use should not be so stringent as to endanger the safety of an investigator.

We have noted tremendous differences in the ways various law-enforcement agen-cies exercise "direct control and supervision" of private undercover agents. Some require that the undercover investigator be thoroughly searched before every drug pur-chase and constantly monitored during the "buy." Although this is an excellent method of supervising street informants during most criminal investigations, it can be overly oppressive during an investigation of drug violations in the workplace. For example, it would seem unnatural if an undercover investigator who was offered the oppor-tunity to buy drugs in a company locker room agreed to the purchase on a condition that the sale take place in the company parking lot, next to a van with mirrored windows.

If law-enforcement becomes comfortable with the agency's level of profession-alism, they may set only general guidelines and provide little supervision. This, how-ever, can damage the credibility of the investigation; without the required control and supervision, the criminal case can be more easily impeached on the grounds that the private investigator had no authority to engage in any illegal acts.

It is also important to remember that law-enforcement agencies are generally reluctant to authorize private investigators as their agents because of genuine concerns about their professionalism and experience. As the law-enforcement community con-tinues to experience manpower problems that affect its ability to respond to problems of substance abuse in the workplace, and as private investigative agencies solidify their reputations for professionalism, cooperative relationships between the two will become more commonplace.

## Electronic Eavesdropping

The use of electronic devices to document transgressions against company policy can be extremely useful during arbitration and litigation subsequent to an investigation, particularly if the truth of an incident is at issue. The two major types of electronic eavesdropping devices are those that record still or moving images and those that record sound.

The most popular format for still images is the 35-millimeter photograph, and videotape has replaced film as the primary format for moving images. For many types of investigations, including drug investigations, moving images are preferred. Today's video recorders not only can record events in both real time and time-lapse but also are capable of dubbing both direct and transmitted audio, which can be very valuable during the taping of a drug buy. In general, as long as image recording is done in public areas, it is not considered an invasion of privacy. This will become an issue, however, when image-recording devices are used in areas such as locker rooms or bathrooms, where most people have a reasonable expectation of privacy.

The use of sound-recording devices can expose private investigators to substantial risks of litigation. Both federal and state laws should be carefully reviewed before the covert recording of sound is undertaken. Most eavesdropping laws fit into one of two categories: those concerning one-party or two-party consent. Generally, federal eavesdropping laws allow one citizen to record or transmit the conversations of others without their consent as long as the citizen who makes the audio recording is present and a party to the recorded conversation (this is a common example of one-party consent). It would be illegal, however, for a citizen to hide a recording or transmitting device in order to eavesdrop on conversations to which he or she is not a party. Both private citizens and law-enforcement agencies that wish to eavesdrop on the conversation of others usually need a court order to do so.

Some state laws are more restrictive than the federal laws. Two-party consent laws almost always require that all parties to any conversation know beforehand that the conversation is to be recorded and/or transmitted. Some states, such as California, allow one-party consent for law-enforcement agents but require two-party consent for citizens. Citizens acting under the direct control and supervision of law-enforcement agencies can revert to the one-party consent guidelines. They can also do this without the permission of California peace officers if they believe that in so doing they will be able to document a felony involving violence, bribery, extortion, kidnapping, or an obscene phone call. The states of Washington and Pennsylvania, however, are among those that require both citizens and law-enforcement agencies to obtain court orders before eavesdropping unless all parties involved consent to such activity. Our advice is to thoroughly research all the laws that may affect eavesdropping in your geographic region.

*False Imprisonment*

In workplace investigations, employee allegations of false imprisonment are most often made during or after an interview or confrontation with the employee. To guard against this allegation, the investigator should never require an employee to remain in an interview room and should be sure to document—in writing, on a tape recording, or both—that the employees' participation in the interview was voluntary. These precautions will be discussed in more detail in chapter 7.

# PART II

## The Five-Phase Program

# Chapter 5

## Phase I: Addressing Clients' Problems and Helping Them Develop Solutions

In our experience, no matter how severe a company's problem of internal theft, drug abuse, or both, it could always be traced to an inadequacy on the part of management to properly screen, train, and supervise employees.

Our clients who had done an adequate job in these areas were not always free of the problems of internal theft or drug abuse on company time and property. If those problems existed, however, they were usually diagnosed quickly—and they were noticeably less extensive than those faced by our clients who had not adequately handled employee screening, training, and supervision. We have found that most companies do a far better job of discussing their goals and standards in these areas of management than of acting to meet them. The reasons for this are simple: it is easier said than done, and talk is cheap.

During the first phase of the five-phase program, in which the investigator first meets with the client, it is important to determine the client's attitudes about employee screening, training, and supervision. Generally, managers seem to recognize the importance of these concepts, but most do not fully practice what they preach. The following questions are helpful during this phase of the interaction between the investigator and the potential client:

May I see a copy of your employment application?

What do you say to your applicants when you give them this application?

Do you give applicants any indication of how thoroughly you will check the information on the application?

Are your interviews and screening handled by a personnel department or by various department heads?

What kind of questions are asked of applicants during job interviews?

What do you feel are the sensitive legal issues that preclude you from asking certain questions, both on the application and during the course of the job interview?

When do you first discuss company rules with applicants?

What company rules do you discuss orally with applicants, and which do you simply give them in writing?

May I have a copy of your company's policies and procedures?

Can you describe the substance and duration of your training program?

Have any of your supervisors ever caught employees committing serious violations of company policies? If so, what were the results of those discoveries?

How equitably do you think your supervisors administer discipline?

Do you think any of your supervisors have violated company rules, either on or off company time and property?

Do your supervisors actively watch for violations of the company's drug and theft policies?

How productive do your supervisors think the work force is?

Through this line of questioning, an investigator should be able to get a good idea of the prospective client's management style. They should also be able to determine how well-managed the company is and, by extension, how serious its problems of theft and substance abuse may be.


## THE CLIENT MEETING: WHO MUST BE THERE

When a company considers instituting an investigation that involves the incursion of operatives into the workplace, as few persons as possible should know about it. Investigative activities, by their very nature, should remain confidential. From many years of experience in handling covert assignments, we know that people who are not trained in clandestine activities generally find it hard to keep an undercover investigation secret. If a company is to avoid the serious consequences of an exposed investigation, it must take steps during the initial planning stage to limit knowledge of the undercover investigation—if not to one person, then to only those individuals who absolutely must know about it.


### The Decision Maker

Who in a company can make the decision to launch an undercover operation varies, depending on the structure of the organization. If the company has a security department, the person in charge of it should under most circumstances be involved in the decision. We can think of two exceptions to this: if members of the security force are suspected of involvement in theft or illegal drug use, or if the department's past conduct raises concerns about its ability to maintain the confidentiality of the investigation. Of course, if the security unit is the primary target of an investigation, it is not made aware of the operation.

Department managers and supervisors who are not suspected of policy violations should not be allowed to conclude that they are. This means that they should eventually be notified of the investigation, but preferably not in the beginning. In any event, they should be informed before the investigation becomes common knowledge in the workplace.

## The Investigator

To be effective, an undercover investigation must be competently planned and controlled from the outset. The agency should send the person best qualified to explain the ramifications of the undercover operation to the initial meeting with a potential client. Generally, this will be an officer of the agency—someone who has authority over the agency's employees and can assume liability for their conduct. This person must be able to answer all questions posed by the decision maker and other members of the client organization concerning problems that may surface.

## The Legal Advisor

As mentioned in chapter 4, the wrongful discharge suit is probably the chief civil litigation risk during any investigation in the workplace. Many corporate attorneys only occasionally deal firsthand with criminal or labor litigation and thus are not always well-versed in those areas of law. Variations in work environments, unions, and local labor laws necessitate that no company embark upon any activity that exposes it to legal risk without sound advice from a competent labor attorney. As a condition of accepting a case, we require each of our clients to do so. The labor attorney should be present to advise the client before, during, and after the undercover investigation into theft or drug abuse. The attorney should certainly be consulted before the employer takes any overt action on the basis of information obtained during the investigation.

## PERCEIVING THE PROBLEM

It is important for the investigator to query the potential client to determine how in touch he or she is with the obvious manifestations of the company's drug-related problem. The main factors to consider, as mentioned earlier, are worker compensation experience-modification ratios, productivity level, shrinkage and absenteeism rates, and effectiveness of quality control. This inquiry will help the investigator to determine whether the company has a serious substance-abuse problem, because substance abuse is often the root cause of significant problems in one or more of the aforementioned areas.

In addition, the response of management to these questions can give the investigator a very good sense of how well the company is managed. For instance, if management has no idea what the company's shrinkage rate is, this may indicate either that the company has no inventory process or that management does not track the available statistics that would reflect a problem. A statistic that is available to all managers is the worker compensation experience-modification ratio. Managers who are unaware of this figure are not on top of one of the most basic administrative functions. Unfortunately, many managers rely on "gut feelings" when it comes to issues of productivity and quality control.

## Rumors

Two methods of communication exist in every work environment: one official, the other unofficial. Official communications usually come from management in the form of newsletters, bulletin-board notices, conferences, and meetings. But often, the most indicative communications of what is really going on in the workplace are the unofficial ones. Long before actual evidence of theft or drug abuse surfaces, rumors of its existence will be heard.

In some cases, rumors are ignored by supervisors and managers because they are not confronted with hard evidence. But ignoring rumors is just another form of denial. Rumors of internal theft and drug use on company time and property are analogous to the smoke that appears just before flames break out. The same supervisors and line managers who would not stand by and ignore smoke in the workplace often ignore rumors of malfeasance within their facilities.

## Anonymous Tips

A world-famous manufacturer of personal computers, with offices and plants located in Santa Clara, California ("Silicon Valley"), was advised by detectives from the San Jose Police Department that personal computers, in unopened boxes bearing the name of the company and the item, were being sold on street corners in the city for eight hundred dollars each. The information had been furnished to the police by informants and anonymous tipsters. The company, riding the crest of the wave in sales of personal computers, refused to believe it had a problem. The situation continued to escalate. Eventually, the police obtained serial numbers that identified some units as having been manufactured but not shipped. The owners were then forced to take the problem seriously.

Preliminary investigation spotlighted some problems on the loading docks at the company's warehouse. Physical surveillance was instituted. In less than a week the case was solved. A wholesale theft ring was subsequently identified and its members were arrested. The ring consisted of warehouse personnel, members of the contract guard force, and independent truck drivers. Controls in the warehouse were found to be so inadequate that the auditors could only estimate that "in excess of $300,000.00 of product [personal computers] could not be accounted for from the records." How much was stolen, and by whom, will probably never be known.

## UNDERSTANDING THE COMPANY ENVIRONMENT

Recently, we interviewed a prospective client concerning serious allegations of employee disloyalty in the company's security department. This problem had hampered the organization's ability to carry out its primary function. All of the disaffection could be traced to one ringleader, a senior security administrator. When asked, "Why don't you either fire him or transfer him?" the client replied, "You don't understand the corporate culture. This company doesn't make mistakes when it hires people. To fire someone means admitting we made a mistake, and transferring him is easier said than done."

If investigators are to do a worthwhile job, it is essential that they have a firm understanding of "the corporate culture"—the company environment. Most investigators who have had experience working in more than one part of the country will agree that an investigative technique that works in one region won't necessarily work in another. Similarly, there are differences between companies. The investigator must ask for information on employee and union relations, demographics, and past problems and punitive actions during the initial interview with the client in order to best understand the company's environment.

### Union Relations

The reaction of organized labor to investigations of internal theft and drug use in the workplace is mixed. Some unions are cooperative; others are not. Most unions support Employee Assistance Programs but usually do not support drug testing in the workplace; some have taken legal action to prevent employers from implementing it (the case of *The Players Association* v. *The National Football League* is one example). Before an investigation begins, the investigator must have a thorough understanding of the company's union relations and how they may affect the work environment.

It is also advisable that the investigator carefully examine the collective bargaining agreement, with particular attention to any clause that is not normally included under the National Labor Relations Act. Two of the most significant (although not necessarily common) bargaining issues relate to discovery and representation. Some companies have agreed to take action against employees within a prescribed period after the employer's discovery of a policy violation (often about ten days). Obviously, it is important to know this in advance of an undercover operation, for failure to comply with the discovery clause would surely be the demise of the investigation.

One of us recently learned this the hard way during a workplace investigation, when the union business agent asked him why the investigators were wasting their time interviewing thieves and drug dealers whose transgressions had been discovered prior to the discovery period of less than two weeks, stipulated in the collective bargaining agreement. Much of the investigation was wasted because only the most recent transgressors could be confronted. Had the discovery clause been noted during the initial client meeting through an examination of the bargaining agreement, the outcome of the investigation would have been much better.

As discussed in chapter 4, the Weingarten law gives all employees covered under a collective bargaining agreement the right to request union representation during an interview that may result in disciplinary action. This is not to be confused with the Miranda law, which applies to citizens being questioned by police in criminal matters, and requires the police to notify interview subjects, before the interview commences, that they have certain rights and can waive them if they want to. Under the Weingarten law, the interviewer is not required to advise employees of their rights, but simply to comply if they exercise those rights. Occasionally, a company agrees, through collective bargaining, to make an exception to this rule. An investigation undertaken without inspection of this aspect of the contract will certainly be headed for disaster.

## Employee Relations

All companies are not, of course, unionized. In a nonunion environment, it is not always easy to tell whether there is an adversary relationship between the employees and the company; nevertheless, the investigator must know. The best source for information on employer-employee relations is the employees themselves. Good employee morale generally translates into good relations, whereas poor morale indicates an adversary relationship with management.

### Major Employee-Relations Issues

*Reasonable Conduct.* Undercover investigative personnel, case managers, and supervisors should act reasonably at all times. The case file should contain written evidence of all the major decisions made with regard to the progress of the case.

*Search and Seizure.* Even at work, there are places where employees can reasonably expect privacy. Such locations as the employees' lockers, desks, and restrooms should be searched only when absolutely necessary and only with the employees' consent and/or prior knowledge.

*Signed Statements.* Statements should always be made freely and voluntarily, never induced by threats or promises. Statements should be in writing and be signed by the employee and a witness. Any issue concerning Weingarten rights should always be resolved in favor of the employee; if the issue is ever adjudicated, this will demonstrate that the employer treated the worker fairly.

*Surveillance.* At certain times and places, no surveillance of any type should be undertaken against an employee. Without a court order, most electronic surveillance should be absolutely forbidden. Any surveillance that may amount to an invasion of privacy (e.g., camera surveillance in an employee restroom) should be forbidden.

*Representation during Interviews.* If at any time during an interview an employee has reason to believe that the result of the interview might be disciplinary action against him or her and requests representation by a member of the union, either grant the employee's request or terminate the interview.

## Employee Demographics

We recently conducted an undercover investigation and a security audit at a prestigious hospital and medical center in southern California. When this facility had first been constructed, the property on which it was located was in a desirable suburban area of a large city. But circumstances had changed; at the time of our survey, the facility was an island surrounded by a ghetto with a high crime rate. This medical center shares a problem with many other organizations that have capital investments in plants and buildings: those structures cannot easily be relocated. If the areas in which their facilities deteriorate, these institutions and firms must simply learn to survive in the altered environment. Such companies have found that it makes good sense, both economically and politically to recruit much of their labor force from the immediate surrounding area. In the absence of a very thorough applicant-screening program, however, these companies have hired more than their fair share of problems. One consequence has been higher-than-average rates of internal theft and drug use on company time and property. The combination of the two, a high-risk exposure due to geographical location and external theft coupled with higher-than-average internal problems, has caused more than one company to consider abandoning its initial concern for capital investment in favor of relocation.

## Past Problems

One of the best indicators of the likelihood of future problems is the empirical data available on past problems. As we often tell our clients, isolated incidents should be handled on a case-by-case basis. Trends, however, mean that something is wrong and must be corrected if the problem is to be solved.

It is certainly safe to predict that unless a company takes a serious approach to the problems of internal theft and drug use on company time and property, these problems will escalate. Therefore, symptoms that may indicate a major problem should not be ignored. We teach our undercover operatives never to underestimate a simple act of theft, such as the pilfering of tools by an employee. People generally don't steal or use drugs openly; they try to conceal such activities. What the operative observes may be just the tip of an iceberg. An employer might state, "Other companies may have these problems in their work force, but not us. Our people are different. We may have some employees who smoke a joint during a break once in a while, but that's a problem everyone has." But again, what the employer has observed may be just the tip of the iceberg.

## Past Punitive Actions

Another predictor of future problems is past punitive actions. The absence of these may actually work to disguise rather than highlight the magnitude of the problem. This was the experience of Dr. Howard Frankel, formerly medical director of Rockwell International, who says he quit that position partly because "management repeatedly gave in to union demands that drug abusers be reinstated in their jobs."[1]

The apparent absence of past incidents of theft or drug use on company time and property, despite the pervasiveness of drug use and crime in the surrounding community, may in itself indicate a need to look for a hidden problem. On the other hand, if sufficient evidence of a problem that affects the surrounding community also exists in the client's facility, the investigator and client can turn to the task of deciding on an approach to solve the problem.

## OVERCOMING THE CLIENT'S DENIAL

Denial, one of the harsh realities of illegal drug use, often affects both the user and those in close relationships with the user (family, friends, coworkers). One of us recently had a discussion with the management of a large midwestern nuclear power plant concerning the issue of random toxicology testing (a prerequisite to unescorted access into most nuclear power facilities). The discussion centered on the issue of illegal drug use by employees as it might affect the safety of the plant and the surrounding community. The plant's management clearly did not believe that there was a drug problem in the workplace, even though the facility was located between two large metropolitan areas where drug abuse was rampant.

It is difficult to overcome denial on the part of the employer. One way to counteract it is to describe to the employer the cases of past clients, in the same business and the same geographical area, who once took the same position but eventually realized that they had a substance-abuse problem on their hands. It is very difficult to convince employers who do not think they have a problem that you can provide them with a solution, but with persistent effort it can sometimes be done.

In fact, successful investigators often find that they can get valuable testimonials from past clients who were originally doubting Thomases but came to realize, through the results of an investigation, that they indeed had a significant problem. We recently had a potential client come to us with all the typical manifestations of a drug problem. The president of the company, however, remained unconvinced that the source of the problem was drug abuse. As we had handled many cases in his industry with a great deal of success, we were able to refer him to other presidents who had once held the same point of view. After they told him how their initial skepticism had dissolved by the end of their investigations, he was more inclined to consider the possibility that a drug problem existed in his workplace.

---

1. Quoted in "Battling the Enemy Within," *Time* (17 March 1986).

Most company managers are never completely convinced they have a problem until the final tally is in. At the outset, it is not necessary for an investigator to completely convince a potential client that he or she has serious problems; it is only necessary to prepare the client for that potential. After all, if the company already knew what its problems were, it would not need to hire an investigator.

## REVIEW OF CURRENT POLICIES

If one is to have faith in the system prescribed in this book, one must accept the premise that a significant portion of the work force is guilty of serious transgressions against company theft and drug policies and will probably be identified as culpable. Therefore, before any investigation commences, the investigator should analyze the company's current policies to make sure they are free of deficiencies. It will be much easier to administer discipline equitably if the company has fair rules.

### The Drug Policy

Amazingly, when we ask managers what their company's current drug policy is, most of them cannot tell us. Even worse, once they dig out the policy to show it to us, we find that it does not meet the current minimum standards for a decent drug policy more than 75 percent of the time.

The most basic drug policy should contain at least the following: "It is a violation of company policy for any employee to sell or buy or offer to sell or buy, possess, use, or be under the influence of any illegal substance on company time and/or on company property." (This covers only illegal substances and not alcohol, which should also be covered in the substance-abuse policy.)

Many clients wonder why it is necessary to use the word *sell* if the policy already states that it is against company policy to *possess* an illegal substance. After all, it is difficult to sell a substance if you do not possess it. The explanation is simple. In many states, the crime of selling a substance occurs at the very moment of the offer, regardless of whether money or drugs actually change hands or, for that matter, whether the deal is ever consummated. Some states address this issue in their conspiracy laws, whereas others (California, for example) address it in their health and safety code or drug laws. It is not uncommon, during a confrontational interview, for an employee to rationalize that he or she merely discussed a drug deal on company time and property; the deal was not consummated until after the employees were off of company time and property. Employers who do business in states with laws that make offering to buy or sell an illegal substance a crime can argue that if the offer was made on company time and property, the employee in effect "sold" on company time and property. To avoid allegations that management's actions against such employees are based on a technicality, it is important that the drug policy state that it is a violation for an employee to sell *or offer to sell* an illegal substance.

We have recently seen cases in which drugs that are not technically illegal substances were sold on company time and property. For example, there are the so-called designer drugs—new drugs created by chemists who slightly alter the molecular structure of drugs that are illegal, as defined by the Uniform Controlled Substance Act. These new substances are often more potent than the originals. Until new drug laws are written, many of them will technically remain legal (although they could be lethal).

Some people sell legal substances such as caffeine (often available in an over-the-counter, nonprescription preparation such as No-Doze) in the workplace. These legal substances are often sold to naive drug users who think they are buying a methamphetamine or cocaine. Since most drug policies cover only illegal substances, many managers think that the sale of legal drugs in the workplace is not an actionable violation. In reality, however, it is automatically against the policy because it is against the law in most states. Also, most state drug laws make it illegal to sell any substance that one represents as being illegal. Thus, employees who sell a substance they say is cocaine when in fact it may be caffeine may be violating the law. To be sure this is clearly communicated in our clients' drug policies, we recommend that they include the following language: "It is a violation of company policy for any employee to sell or buy or offer to sell or buy, possess, use, or be under the influence of any illegal substance *or any substance that is purported to be illegal.*"

Another important issue to consider is the purchase of illegal drugs. In most states there are no separate statutes covering drug purchase; both the buyer and seller are guilty of "selling." Nonetheless, *buy* is another good word to include in a company drug policy.

What if an employee did not sell or buy, but simply provided, or was provided, an illegal substance free of charge? Once again, most state drug laws do not make the exchange of money the determining factor as to whether a sale was consummated; providing is considered the same as selling. The logic is that the provider of the illegal substance has received some benefit in exchange, even if only in friendship. *Providing* is therefore another excellent word to include in a company drug policy. As you can see, the point of a good drug policy is to address both the minor and major issues so that there is no room for mininterpretation or confusion.

Now for the most elusive concept: What is "under the influence"? This question has caused much debate recently. In chapter 10 Dr. Raymond Kelly discusses toxicology—the science that in our opinion offers the only logical approach to determining whether an employee is under the influence of a substance at a given time. At this writing, there is no published legal definition of "under the influence" except for the scale of blood-alcohol levels in the motor vehicle code. In time this may change. Meanwhile, employers would be well advised to develop drug-testing policies that are as fair as possible to their employees.

Many employers erroneously assume that drug testing can prove whether or not someone is under the influence of a substance. In reality, it can only indicate that an individual probably consumed or used the substance in question at some time.

Urine testing is an excellent method for identifying drug use because the metabolites of many drugs are present for longer periods of time in the urine than in the blood. We recommend that our clients use urinalysis for preemployment screening of applicants and that they analyze both the urine and blood of employees subjected to drug testing to ensure fairness.

For example, if an employee who regularly uses marijuana on the weekend were subjected to a urine test on a Friday, the active component of the drug, tetrahydrocannabinol (THC), might be detected. The test result would thus be positive, even though it would be highly unlikely for the employee to still be under the influence of the drug. However, if a blood test given to the same employee at the same time detected significant levels of THC (over one hundred nanograms per milliliter), it could reasonably be argued that the employee was under the influence at the time, because THC is metabolized more quickly out of the circulatory system than it is out of the urinary system. The point here is to develop a policy that will be envisioned as fair to a reasonable person. A section of the drug policy should explain all the drug-testing methods that may be used by the employer to determine any employee's fitness for duty.

A word of caution: many states have, or are developing, new laws regarding drug testing by employers. Civil libertarians argue that drug testing is an invasion of a citizen's basic right to privacy. Employers argue that it is the only logical way to ensure a safe and drug-free work environment. Most states have laws that protect the confidentiality of drug-test results, which are often considered medical information. Regulations vary from state to state and change periodically, so we advise employers to obtain competent labor counsel on the subject.

As you can see, a lot of thought must go into the creation of a good drug policy that is fair to employees, protects the employer, and fits the employer's needs and philosophies. There really is no "boilerplate" policy that will work for everyone in every state.

## The Theft Policy

Unbelievable though it may be, we have actually come across clients who did not have an official theft policy. They reasoned that most employees do not normally steal from their employers. Although we agree, it is still prudent for employers to provide their employees with a clearly stated policy on theft. Most reasonable people understand that to steal is to take property belonging to someone else without his or her knowledge, consent, or permission. The workplace, however, gives rise to some interesting rationalizations.

Many employees who have stolen company property rationalize that they were only "borrowing" it with the intent to return it at a later date; it is simply an unfortunate coincidence that they have been caught with the merchandise before they had an opportunity to return it. "Borrowing," however, implies that someone with the requisite authority has given permission for the merchandise to be removed from the premises—a point that most thieves who use this rationale fail to consider. A well-thought-out theft policy could certainly address this issue. All employees should be clearly informed that no merchandise may be removed from company premises without formal permission. In addition, the company can institute a property-removal documentation system, which generally works best if more than one manager is required to pre-approve the removal of any property.

Another common rationalization for theft is "the company was going to throw it away." When this is true, the property-removal process just described will apply. But allowing the removal of "damaged" or "junk" merchandise can set a dangerous precedent. We have seen perfectly good merchandise deliberately damaged by an employee who wanted to justify its subsequent removal to management. The best policy is to make it clear to employees that they are not entitled to take home damaged merchandise.

It is also important that the theft policy indicate what constitutes theft in terms of the dollar value of property or merchandise taken without permission. Pilferage is often not considered by employees (or even management) as outright theft. But if a company sets a precedent of only taking disciplinary action against employees who steal over fifty dollars' worth of merchandise, workers may get the message that it's okay to steal $49.99 a day! The best value to set for theft is one cent; what constitutes theft can then be judged on a case-by-case basis. Remember, a written rule can quickly be rendered meaningless if management practices something different than it preaches.

## Employee Assistance Programs

It is important for the investigator to determine whether the client company or its union has an employee assistance program (EAP). The purpose of an EAP is to identify, motivate, rehabilitate, and follow up on employees with three problems: alcohol or drug abuse or addiction, emotional or family problems, and financial and legal problems. These programs use the concepts of wellness, safety, benefits, and medical assistance to approach serious problems affecting the work force.

We are strong advocates of the proper use of a well-thought-out EAP. Companies that afford employees an opportunity to come forward and seek help for their problems without fear of reprisal will have gone a long way to convince its workers that management is truly concerned about their well-being. Certainly, if an investigation at such a company were to catch a significant number of employees transgressing against the rules, the remaining employees would be more apt to say, "The company had a strong and clear rule, they communicated it well to us, and they offered all employees the opportunity to come forward for help, without fear of reprisal. Those who did not come forward and seek help from the company therefore deserve their punishment."

Unfortunately, EAPs are sometimes misapplied. Companies that adopt the policy of helping employees who come forward and then also help those who are "caught" set a dangerous precedent. Why should employees who have problems and need help draw undue scrutiny to themselves if the company has a reputation for giving the same kind of assistance to those who come forward as to those who get caught?

We feel strongly that employees who do not take advantage of employee assistance before they are caught should be treated in a much different fashion. That is not to say that all such employees should be fired. The majority of professional rehabilitators agree that the most important thing to do initially is to ensure that these workers have overcome their denial of their problems and faced the fact that they need help from an outside source to cope with the problem. Once this is accomplished, rehabilitators often provide some sort of support to help the employee deal with the problem.

If a company discovers that an employee has a substance-abuse problem without that employee coming forward on his or her own, it will either fire the worker or give him or her one or more opportunities to attempt to resolve the problem. If a company chooses the latter course, this will have less of a negative impact on the work force than requiring the employee to enter the EAP as a condition of continued employment. The company should also put the employee on probation (although many labor attorneys prefer not to use that term), the conditions of which should not be that the worker enter the EAP but that he or she end the problem behavior and submit to random drug testing. We also firmly believe that if the employee feels that he or she cannot meet the terms of the probation, the company should allow him or her to enter the EAP on a voluntary basis.

## Amnesty

Before launching an undercover investigation, an employer may want to offer amnesty to any employee who is involved in drug abuse on company time and property. Amnesty allows employees to come forward, confess their problems, and receive treatment. It is a sincere outreach to those in need of help. It is not, and should never be allowed to become, a law-enforcement trap. Amnesty should be offered for a specific time period (say, 30 days) and then ended. It should be widely publicized among the work force, on all shifts, and in every department. With some modifications, amnesty can also be applied to theft situations.

Amnesty, if it fits in with the overall corporate philosophy, can be effective for several reasons. It allows employees to come forth with their problems and obtain treatment and rehabilitation through the EAP. An amnesty campaign usually satisfies the union (if one exists), the labor commission, and any other arbitrating body that the employer acted in accordance with the implied covenant of good faith and fair dealing, should that ever become an issue during a subsequent hearing.

## Past Enforcement

It is very important that the investigator learn to what extent the company's written and communicated policies are enforced. If management establishes a track record for being either too lenient or too stringent in administering discipline for violations of written policy, a plaintiff's attorney can make a good case for the invalidation of such policy.

Does this mean that if a company has not abided by its own policies it is forever destined to live in fear that they will be judged invalid? The answer is no, so long as the company simply acknowledges what the policy has been and how it has typically been enforced until the present and documents any changes management wishes to institute.

## The "Henceforth" Memo

Management has the right to change its rules and how they are enforced whenever it deems appropriate. As long as these changes are legal and well communicated, the risk of negative repercussions is minimal.

If the enforcement of company policy is to be changed, it is important that management distribute a "henceforth" memo to all employees, completely explaining how the old rules had been enforced in the past, stating the company's intention to institute a new enforcement policy, and explaining the reason for the change. A form should be attached for every employee to sign to indicate that he or she has read and understood the new policy. If changes are made in the rules as well, those changes should also be documented in the memo, and all new employees should sign the attached form until the company's procedure manual has been revised to reflect the changes.

### The Importance of Postponing Changes in the Workplace after Amnesty

The employer should be cautioned to avoid making any changes in the workplace immediately after an amnesty campaign. Doing so might alert those who remain drug users, drug sellers, or thieves that an investigation is forthcoming. It is better to let the dust settle and the wrongdoers to again become complacent during a cooling-off period (usually a few months at the most). The undercover operative is inserted into the work force during this period to become acclimated to the environment and acquainted with the employees before engaging in any probative investigative activity (we refer to this as the getting-established mode). A note of caution: the employer and investigator should always weigh the issue of a safe work environment against the benefit of the cooling-off period, as there could be a liability issue if someone were injured as the result of a drug-related accident during this time.

## FIDELITY INSURANCE RESEARCH

Most firms that underwrite business insurance often include fidelity insurance as part of the package. Fidelity insurance usually comes in the form of a blanket bond that insures a company against thefts by employees. For many claims, the company does not have to determine who committed a theft as long as it can prove that the loss occurred.

Before an undercover operation commences, it is important that the investigator, in conjunction with the client's risk manager or insurance broker, determine whether the company currently has a fidelity policy and, if so, what its benefits are. It's amazing how many companies have this coverage without realizing it. A sizable recovery of money through fidelity insurance can often more than make up for the cost of an investigation. We also recommend that the client seek the advice of legal counsel with regard to fidelity insurance claims after the investigation.

Most crime-insurance programs begin with "3D" coverage (comprehensive dishonesty, disappearance, and destruction insurance—a blanket crime policy or broadform storekeepers' policy). This coverage usually reimburses a company for losses due to employee dishonesty or counterfeit currency, as well as for loss of money, securities, or merchandise through robbery, burglary, or mysterious disappearance. These policies also generally cover certain types of check forgery and damage to the premises or equipment as the result of a break-in. A deductible is commonly associated with "3D" insurance to exclude small, frequent losses from coverage. This reduces the insurance premium and limits coverage to large, serious losses.

## Structure the Investigation to Meet Subrogation, Discovery, and Mysterious Disappearance Clauses

Insurance companies that underwrite fidelity insurance for employers often require that they be informed of a breach of fidelity within a prescribed period of time from the time of its discovery. If one of the investigative goals is proof of insurable loss, then the terms of the policy and conditions of coverage must be met.

A subrogation clause is usually included in fidelity insurance policies to protect the insurance carrier from actions on the part of the insured that might interfere with the carrier's ability to recover its losses from any responsible parties. It is therefore important to read this clause carefully before conducting an investigation so that nothing will be done that might invalidate the policy. When in doubt, check with both the labor attorney and insurance broker for advice.

As mentioned before, the mysterious disappearance clause sometimes allows an employer to file a fidelity insurance claim without actually being certain of who perpetrated a theft. This does not necessarily mean that the insurance company will gladly pay the insured employer simply because he or she believes that a theft occurred. Most carriers require a very detailed proof-of-loss statement to support such a claim. It is therefore crucial that a company have good inventory-control documentation if it is to take advantage of its insurance policy's mysterious disppearance clause.

## EXPOSED INVESTIGATIONS

Investigations, both overt and covert, can be beset by unexpected problems. The old saw "proper planning prevents poor performance" is as true in the business of investigation as it is in any other calling. Even in routine assignments, investigators must plan for a variety of contingencies so that they can deal with them if and when they do occur. A problem of particular significance is the exposure of an undercover investigation.

With proper planning, an investigative agency should usually be able to conclude an investigation to the employers' satisfaction without anyone else in the work force ever knowing about it. The "blown cover"—the worst nightmare of every professional investigator—rarely happens in a professionally managed undercover program. When it happens, it is usually because either the cover itself was not well prepared or an unqualified investigator was given the job and not supervised adequately. Perhaps the investigator was overzealous and tried to get information too quickly, or the employer simply told too many people about the investigation, either deliberately or unwittingly.

## How to React to "Shots in the Dark"

Occasionally, especially if a company's work force has been the subject of successful undercover investigations in the past, an employee might confront an undercover investigator. In such a situation, the best course of action for the investigator is simply to deny any knowledge or involvement in the operation. The technique of using reverse psychology also tends to work well in these cases. For example, an undercover operative could confront the confronters and accuse them of being investigors to remove suspicion from himself.

## How and When to Inform Unions of Investigations

At the outset, the investigator should learn as much as possible about the history of the relationship between management and the union. No matter how good that relationship may be, officers of the union should not be treated any differently than other members of management who do not need to know the details of an undercover investigation.

Often, when the relationship between management and the union is particularly good, there is a temptation to advise the union of the investigation so as to make it "part of the team." Sometimes this is done out of fear that the union might become militant if it learns of the "spying" activities at a later date. But it is rarely, if ever, advisable to bring officers of the union into the inner circle at the inception of an investigation. It is usually best to advise the union of the investigation at the time of confrontation, when management will have developed the greatest justification for their action and therefore the best defense. If confrontational interviews with employees are not necessary, there is rarely a reason for the union to be advised of the investigation.

It is our experience that unions have become quite practical in their attitude toward investigations. One union business agent recently told us and our client that he was glad he had not known about the investigation in his company until it was over, for if he had he would have felt compelled to disclose it to the rank and file.

No two unions will react to an investigation in the same fashion. We are sure some union officials may be willing to work closely with management in the pursuit of information through an undercover investigation. Nevertheless, we still believe that the most prudent course is to be conservative and only disclose the facts of an investigation to individuals who have a need to know.

We strongly recommend that no investigator attempt to deal with unions on a professional level unless he or she has a thorough education in the National Labor Relations Act. This is one area in which investigators can stray too far outside of their professional expertise and get both themselves and their clients in a great deal of trouble. If an investigative agency does not have a great deal of experience in dealing with unions, it is best that it bring in professionals who understand the restrictions of the National Labor Relations Act. This is truly an area for a specialist.

Although unions are not as powerful today as they were ten to twenty years ago, investigators should not be lulled into thinking that unions are completely ineffective. Like any other type of organization, some are led ineptly, but some are managed very professionally. Some employers still consider unions the enemy, but more and more unions—in the interest of survival—are searching for common ground on which to meet management.

Most unions will not countenance employee involvement in drugs and theft. A professionally run union should be willing to support management's efforts to eliminate these problems. Still, some unions take an adversary position when they sit down at the bargaining table with management to chart policies for dealing with employee violations.

## INVESTIGATIVE TECHNIQUES AND OPTIONS FOR THE CLIENT

After the investigator has collected enough information from the client to fully identify the problem, he or she can proceed to discussing possible solutions. Many investigative techniques may be used to solve a given problem, and it may be necessary to discuss all of these with the employer to give him or her a broad view of the options. The decision as to which technique should be used to solve the problem, however, should not be made by most employers. The solution should be proposed by the investigator and approved by the employer, not the reverse. This is the only way to minimize problems in the investigation, not the least of which may be legal liability. After all, employers hire professionals for their expertise; not to avail themselves of that expertise simply does not make sense.

Also, if an investigator allows the employer to dictate what techniques to use and the investigation's results do not meet the employer's expectations, the agency will almost surely be blamed for the failure. The employer will most likely take the position (and justly so) that he or she had the right to expect the investigator not only to suggest the proper method of conducting the investigation but also to insist on using that method in spite of the employer's opposition, even to the point of declining to take or continue the case. This is exactly what we recommend; any other approach is less than professional. The following example will suffice to explain our position.

While conducting a security survey at a private hospital in Los Angeles, one of us discovered an ongoing embezzlement in the accounts receivable department. It became necessary to stop the survey at that point and recommend to the administrator that he contact a private investigator to conduct an interview. The accounts receivable department was small—only five people—and the thefts had all occurred on the same shift in an area where only one cashier had access to the money. The amount stolen was about six thousand dollars. All an investigator would need to do would be to conduct an interview, confront the suspect with the evidence, and hopefully obtain a confession. But the first investigative agency the client called recommended that the client create another position in the accounts receivable department and staff it with an undercover operative for the next six months in order to catch the thief.

The cost to the client for the services of this undercover operative would have been about twelve thousand dollars—double the initial loss. And worse, the chance that the operative would have actually caught the thief red-handed was almost nil because embezzlers seldom steal in the presence of other employees. One could only wonder if the investigative agency was really trying to solve the client's problem or merely trying to sell undercover services. We advised the client to reject this offer in favor of a more realistic, professional, and cost-effective approach to solving the problem.

## Background Investigations

Complete books have been written on the subject of background investigations. The same techniques of background investigation used by personnel departments for hiring purposes may be used by investigators to obtain information about a client's employees during an investigation. The purpose of this section is not to teach the process of background investigation but merely to bring its importance to the reader's attention. The four checks listed below are basic to any background investigation. Because federal and state guidelines and laws may affect such investigations, we recommend that the investigator obtain counsel from a labor attorney before conducting or initiating a background check.

### Credit Checks

Credit information can be revealing, especially in regard to suspected embezzlers and drug abusers. Both types of offenders tend to have expensive habits and are not above stealing moneys from their employers. Most companies have credit departments that have established accounts with credit-reporting agencies. A word of advice: do not advise a credit-reporting agency that you are conducting a background investigation for personnel purposes, even though this is not illegal. If you do, they may reject your inquiry. The reason is that many have had clients whose misuse of credit information resulted in litigation against the credit bureau.

Many companies do not check the credit references of applicants. They say they do not care whether an employee pays his or her bills on time; their concern is whether the person can perform the job for which he or she is being considered. But there is a wealth of revealing information in a credit report, once one learns to read between the lines and decipher the symbols. One of the great advantages of a credit investigation is that it may yield information that was not volunteered by an applicant. For example, say that an applicant once listed a former employer on a credit application and was subsequently discharged by that employer because she violated a company rule. The applicant chooses not to list this former employer on her job application. A credit check may well be the prospective employer's only means of discovering the omission.

The Fair Credit and Reporting Act requires requestors of credit information to obtain permission from employment applicants to release information. Other regulations affect the providers and receivers of credit information if it is to be used against the applicant.

## Criminal Checks

Usually, criminal checks must be limited to information on convictions for crimes. This information is available as a public record. Often, the best source of information on whether a person has been convicted of a crime is the subject himself or herself. If it is not possible or desirable to question the subject, the next best source of information is the alphabetical index of criminal cases at the county courthouse (usually in the office of the clerk of the superior court). This works best if the subject was born and raised in the community where the investigation is taking place. With individuals who have moved frequently in their adult lives, it may be necessary to hire an agency that specializes in processing criminal checks in all known areas of a subject's prior residence.

## Department of Motor Vehicle Checks

A good source of legally obtainable information is a driver's-license check through the state department of motor vehicles. This is especially significant in investigating alcohol and drug abusers, whose life-styles tend to spill over into their driving habits. We know of one airline that used this technique several years ago to identify pilots with alcohol-abuse problems. The pilots were required to take semiannual physical examinations to remain certified to fly by the company and the Federal Aviation Administration. It was simple for the alcohol abusers to abstain from the use of alcohol just prior to the semiannual physical and resume drinking once they were certified. A check of driver's-license records, however, revealed that some of these pilots had come to the attention of the police for driving under the influence of alcohol. If this had occurred more than once, the company arranged a meeting attended by the pilot and people who could bear witness to his or her alcohol problem. The pilot was confronted with the evidence and given a choice: treatment or termination.

## Previous Employment Checks

Personnel offices are poor sources of information on workers' past employment. A better source is the employee's past supervisors. Telephone calls made directly to former supervisors can often reveal information not otherwise obtainable. The process is simple. Just tell the supervisor you are thinking of hiring the subject and ask if he or she would want that person to return as an employee. If the supervisor hesitates, say that he or she can simply state, "I'd rather not answer that question." If the supervisor chooses to give this response, you have all the information you need. On the other hand, few supervisors will hesitate to recommend a former employee who has served well.

## Physical Surveillance

Physical surveillance is a good technique to consider when the work force is so small that inserting an undercover operative would create undue suspicion. At other times physical surveillance can be used to protect the identity of an undercover operative who has gathered information concerning a planned theft or drug buy. The investigator simply establishes the surveillance, or stakeout, of the activity, and once it is consummated, moves in and makes the arrest (this is known as catching the thieves flagrante delicto). Physical surveillance can also be used to corroborate information previously received from any source that one wishes to keep confidential. Oftentimes it is used on a spot-check basis just to ensure that people are doing what they are supposed to do, in the absence of information to the contrary.

Physical surveillance, with or without video aids (cameras), is often recommended to check on route-delivery drivers to ensure that they are delivering merchandise to bona fide customers. This is especially worthwhile for small companies whose delivery drivers often load their own trucks, with or without assistance from warehouse employees. When surveillance is instituted, the investigator is furnished copies of the drivers' daily manifests, which show delivery points and list customers' names, addresses, and items of merchandise. If a driver deviates from the itinerary and makes stops to deliver merchandise not shown on the manifest, this is reported by the investigator. The technique can be used to target a suspected driver or group of drivers at random or to audit selected drivers to ensure that they adhere to established guidelines for on-the-road conduct. It also should be noted that since surveillance is often passive it rarely "proves" but rather provides indications of violations during drug investigations.

We have a few words of caution regarding physical surveillance as an investigative technique. First, it is time-consuming. Any investigative technique that is time-consuming is also expensive. Also, it takes trained operatives, often working in pairs with radio communication, to accomplish surveillance safely without compromising the investigation. Finally, although many investigators know the principles of conducting physical surveillance, few have actually had experience in applying those principles.

## Electronic Eavesdropping Surveillance

As discussed earlier, there are few jurisdictions where electronic eavesdropping can be practiced legally by a private investigative agency working alone. This technique can generally be used only when working with a law-enforcement agency equipped with a court order and the technical expertise to place the recording equipment, microphones, and monitors in a concealed manner. Legal issues aside, it takes a lot of time, manpower, and know-how to properly install and monitor electronic surveillance equipment. For these reasons, we rarely use or recommend this technique.

A technique we do use and recommend, although under strictly controlled circumstances only, is the wearing of a "wire"—a voice-sensitive microphone wired to a tape recorder or transmitter hidden in the operative's clothing. This can be done during the confrontation (or "sting") part of the operation to obtain corroborating evidence (this phase will be explained in detail later in this book).

Again, a word of caution: use of the wire has been overdramatized in every crime story on television. This technique should be used with the utmost caution and only in well-controlled environments. Should the presence of the wire be discovered, a response force must be immediately available to protect the operative. The wire can be a valuable aid in an investigation. Its legality, however, can be an issue in some jurisdictions. Evidence obtained lawfully with a wire is generally admissible in legal proceedings. State laws should be thoroughly reviewed before a wire or any other covert recording equipment is used.

## Interviews with "Friendlies"

It should not be assumed that everyone who works for a living has an adversary relationship with his or her employer. There are people in the work force who, upon being identified as "friendlies," can be approached cautiously for information on inside activities.

Interviews with such employees should be conducted on a highly selective basis and always on neutral ground, or at least away from the workplace. Prior to an interview with a friendly employee, the investigator should review that person's personnel file and perform credit and criminal checks (where legal) to avoid running into any surprises. A friendly insider's furnishing of information to an investigator can often add another dimension to an undercover investigation that might otherwise not be available.

When used as described above, friendlies should be handled like all other informants. No information about the operation should be revealed to them. Even when their motives are completely honest, their lack of training can cause them to make mistakes that could destroy the investigation.

The identity of any undercover operative who is working in conjunction with an employee ("live") informant must be kept confidential at all costs. The live informant cannot have even the merest hint that there is an undercover operative in the work force.

## Surprise Inspections

Alarmed by reports of widespread drug and alcohol use at a remote generating station in Nevada, a public utility organized its own raid. Company managers and security officers cut the personal padlocks off of four hundred employee lockers and conducted searches of the contents. Cars in the parking lot were searched, as were several suspect employees. Seven employees were fired for possession of drugs and alcohol at work in violation of company rules.[1] 

Surprise or random inspections can have a deterrent effect when conducted as described above. Improperly conducted, however, they can have serious negative effects on the morale of employees who are not involved in wrongdoing. Employees who are not suspect should not be led to believe that they are. The "Dragnet" approach, while perhaps an effective way to catch some errant employees, can usually be used only once. In our experience, surprise inspections often serve only to drive problems underground. They don't stop alcohol and drug abuse in the workplace; they just force the targeted workers to be more clever. One should always consider the costs of such operations as well as their long-term benefits and consequences before initiating them.

### Random, or Unannounced, Drug Testing

Probably no more controversial issue exists today than the random, or unannounced, drug test. It was once thought of as the ultimate deterrent. Today, the subject of random testing of body fluids is at issue in every forum available to the debating public. Conservatives take the position that illegal drug use is a safety issue and that random drug testing should be allowed in the public interest. Civil libertarians take the position that such tests are an invasion of privacy as well as an illegal search and seizure, the evidence of which cannot legally be used against the persons tested. Which side will win remains to be seen. The trend, however, appears to be on the side of the civil libertarians. For example, in San Francisco, California, the city council passed an ordinance forbidding random testing. The issue won't be finally decided, however, until the Supreme Court of the United States rules on it.

If random drug testing is used in the workplace, a few simple precautions should be taken to ensure the validity of the test results. The first is supervison of the collection of body fluids (usually urine). A black market for clean urine was developed by employees at one facility in order to circumvent the testing procedure. Because urine was usually collected in the privacy of a restroom, it was simple for employees to provide samples of clean urine that they carried on their person in anticipation of random testing. To counter such a circumvention, a simple test for warmth may be instituted (although such a test is not entirely foolproof, as it is relatively easy to add warmth to a sample). A cold specimen should always be viewed with suspicion.

The testing should be done by a qualified toxicologist who has demonstrated experience in both testing and testifying as an expert witness in administrative and judicial proceedings related to drug and alcohol use.

### Drug-Sniffing Dogs

It has been known for many years that dogs have a much more acute sense of smell than human beings. For this reason, the use of drug-sniffing dogs has become popular

---

1. "Battling the Enemy Within," *Time* (17 March 1986).

with some managers as a method of detecting drugs in the workplace. Although it is an effective method in terms of results and cost, it is not the first detection method we would recommend. The negative aspects of using dogs need to be carefully weighed.

First, the use of dogs is not a covert act. Everyone in the work force will know when it occurs unless it happens after hours. In fact, it is our opinion that unless there is an overriding issue of public safety, dogs should generally be used only after hours. One of the best reasons for this is employee safety. An employee's behavior around the animals could result in an unfortunate biting incident.

If dogs are to be used, the company must ensure that it is protected against litigation for invasion of privacy by covering the use of dogs in its written policy. The policy should state that the employer may use dogs to detect drugs and has the right to search any area that the dogs indicate may contain drugs, including employees' lockers and desks.

## Polygraph Testing

There has been a tremendous amount of litigation revolving around the use of the polygraph in both the private and public sectors. The former has experienced dramatic legislated limitations, even since this book was first conceived. Appendix A has been dedicated to this important legislation. To the degree that the polygraph can be legally used in the private sector, practitioners should nevertheless proceed cautiously. There is a significant sentiment in the United States that polygraph testing, especially used randomly and without cause, may be an invasion of an individual's reasonable expectation of privacy.

As a result the use of the polygraph has become controversial, even among veteran investigators. We, the authors, are split on this issue; one is for, the other against. But we can agree on one last word: in our opinion, the best polygraph examiners are first and foremost experts in the art of interviewing and interrogation. Most of the excellent polygraph examiners we have worked with are able, more than 50 percent of the time, to extract the needed information from a subject without ever hooking that person up to the instrument. If a polygraph examination is to be used in an investigation, we strongly recommend hiring the best examiner available to conduct the inquiry. If an examiner with an outstanding record is not available in the immediate vicinity, we recommend importing one, preferably from a city in the same state to ensure that he or she is conversant with local law.

## Undercover Operations

Properly used, the undercover operation (the focus of chapter 6) can be a very cost-effective investigative technique. This has been found to be especially true in cases of internal theft and illegal drug abuse on company time and property. Improperly used, the undercover operation can be a waste of both time and money and, worse, may involve both the agency and the client in costly litigation. We strongly urge prospective clients to use caution when engaging the services of an investigative agency to conduct an undercover investigation. The best course of action is to thoroughly screen the agency prior to entering into an agreement for such services.

The agency should be able to furnish references—the names of former clients in the same (or similar) business and geographical area as the prospective client. The agency should also be able to furnish the names of labor attorneys and labor consultants with whom it has worked as added assurance that the investigators are conversant with federal and local labor laws. In most investigations, great care must be taken to avoid costly lawsuits over such labor issues as the invasion of privacy and wrongful discharge (chapter 8 covers the discharge or retention of employees after an investigation). The methods used to identify and discipline errant employees in the workplace must be able to withstand the scrutiny of labor commissions and the courts. Any investigative agency not equipped to ensure this is doing itself and its clients a disservice.

## Police Investigations

If the police become involved in an investigation, the investigator should discuss the pertinent criminal issues with the client to minimize surprises and misunderstandings. The client must be told how the police or district attorney approach the prosecution of illegal drug-related activities (more on this in the upcoming section on law-enforcement liaison). This is essential to ensuring that the investigation comes off smoothly and to the client's satisfaction. For example, upon learning that the police will not cooperate in the investigation if the client is not sympathetic to the prosecution issues (for example, litigation over the sale of one marijuana cigarette), the client may not want the investigator to buy drugs from employees during the investigation.

Rarely do employers understand the police's criteria for prosecuting drug-abusing employees. Rarely do police officers understand the complexities of the labor laws with which employers must comply. If an investigator has knowledge of both of these areas, he or she can serve as an excellent mediator between these two groups, which often have diametrically opposed goals. The primary goal of management should be to rid the company of employees who are serious violators of company policy without getting sued in the process. Police officers are charged with enforcing the law and measure their success in numbers of prosecutable cases; they are rarely interested in assisting companies with the enforcements of company rules. Likewise, employers are seldom interested in enforcing the laws of the state.

The investigator should explain to the client the basic concepts of what police departments need to have a successul prosecution. Many managers do not realize that obtaining an employee's confession of violating company rules and the law does not necessarily mean that he or she will be successfully prosecuted. Most states require the police department to bring evidence to the prosecuting attorney that will establish the elements of the crime independent of the confession of the perpetrator.

A good investigator will also meet with the police department and explain the complexities of the labor laws that affect employers on a day-to-day basis. Many police officers do not understand that employers can no longer fire employees simply because they have broken the law. In most states an employer must first prove that the violation of the law was directly related to the workplace. Most often, the illegal act must also have been committed on company time, company property, or both. The concept that employers can be sued by employees for wrongful discharge is also foreign to many police officers.

The investigator should also point out to the employer that the police department does not have the manpower to react quickly to every employer's request for help. For this very reason, the police are reluctant to become involved in any kind of workplace investigation unless they are assured that the company will support them in prosecuting employees guilty of illegal acts. Far too often, police departments have helped companies gather enough proof to fire certain employees, only to find that the company had decided it did not want to see those employees prosecuted.

Morally, most good citizens will support the concept that someone who violates the law should be prosecuted. Practically speaking, however, in many states the prosecution of employees can be fruitless, especially in light of the trend for the criminal justice system to accelerate the handling of cases. It can also be expensive if the employer is sued for false arrest, intentional infliction of emotional distress, entrapment or coercion.

We always recommend to our clients they carefully consider the return on investment before taking steps toward prosecuting employees. The main benefit of prosecuting is the message it sends to the remaining work force. The aforementioned pitfalls, however, may outweigh the advantages. Nonetheless, the best way to prove that an employee is selling drugs is to buy drugs from that employee, and no state allows private investigators to buy, use, or possess illegal substances without first becoming agents of the police. A private investigator's participation in such activities without being under the direct control and supervision of a dully sworn peace officer could nullify the investigation and get the investigator and client arrested.

If prosecution will not result in a great return on the employer's investment, how can a company convince the police to work with it for the purpose of identifying the culprits without promising the police they will prosecute at the end of the case? The answer is that it probably can't.

We have found that if an employer is interested in proving that drug sales are being made on company time and property, it is best to convince him or her to give up the "right" to make a decision concerning prosecution. Technically, the police do not need the permission of the employer to file a case against a culpable employee once a crime is consummated, especially if it is a felony (which drug sale is in most states). But district attorneys are not nearly as attracted to cases involving uncooperative employers as they are to those involving cooperative ones.

We will not accept a drug-related case in which our client desires drug buys to be made unless the client agrees to let the police decide whether or not to prosecute. When we meet with police officials and then subsequently with prosecutors, we are thus able to convince them of the full cooperation of the employer.

Later in this chapter, we will further discuss how the investigative agency should interact with the police to optimize the chance that they will be cooperative. We should note, however, that even if an agency has followed all our recommendations, the police may be reluctant to get involved unless that agency has a good reputation and significant experience in the field of drug investigations and purchases.

## CONTRACT CONSIDERATIONS

### Time Frame

The time frame for investigations of illegal drug-related activity in the workplace averages four to six months. Controlling factors can be the size of the work force and its complacency, the skill of the investigator, and how well the investigation is structured. Some other variables may be involved as well.

It takes approximately thirty to sixty days for an undercover investigator to gain enough of the confidence of dishonest employees to infiltrate possible conspiracies, depending on the number of departments and employees in the company. Once this has been accomplished, another thirty to sixty days are generally needed to complete the undercover investigation and plan for the confrontational interviews of the malefactors. Interviewing usually takes two to three days in the average-sized company. More time may be needed in larger companies. Phase IV of the program (discharge or retention of employees) and Phase V (preventing the problem from recurring) generally take one day each to complete.

### Costs

Costs vary from agency to agency. The general rule of thumb is that costs are dictated by the availability of manpower in the labor market to which the agency has access, coupled with variables that affect the length of a case, such as the extent of the client's problem.

Most agencies are paid for investigations at an hourly rate that covers a minimum guaranteed income for the operative who performs the undercover job. The operative's income includes payment by the employer for duties performed as an employee of the company during the investigation, and payment by the agency for activities conducted as an undercover investigator.

In most jurisdictions the undercover operative is also entitled to time and a half or double time when required to work additional hours to complete an assignment. This can and should be controlled. For example, overtime should initially be limited to instances in which the undercover operative must attend social functions, after the normal workday, for investigative purposes. The investigative agency should have an agreement with the client setting a limit on overtime (say, ten hours) unless permission is obtained to raise the limit. It is well to have a written agreement among all parties that states, "prior to the operative incurring additional overtime or expenses, approval must be obtained from the supervisor, through the employer, before the overtime is incurred.''

Other expenses associated with investigations include the costs of typing the undercover operative's reports; payments to investigators engaged in case management, supervision, and control activities, including meetings with the police and the client; and the operative's apartment rent (if applicable) and travel expenses. Some investigative agencies have a rate sheet that lists the various investigative services and their costs. It is important that the investigator thoroughly explain all such cost considerations to the client before beginning the investigation. It is also advisable to mention to the client a principle that every investigator knows but few articulate: There are no guarantees. It is a mistake for either the client or the investigator to have preconceived ideas about the course or outcome of any investigation. The entire process is one of discovery. As the facts of a case unfold and trends develop, one may make certain predictions—but not before.

The use of the interview-team approach (described in chapter 7) is generally billed to the client at a higher hourly rate because it involves highly sophisticated investigative techniques. It is also the phase of an investigation in which the client and investigative agency are at greatest risk for allegations that could lead to civil litigation. The employer should understand that only seasoned investigators with a firm foundation in civil and labor law should be allowed to conduct interviews. Investigators with this level of training and experience generally command higher pay than those who are less qualified.

We often hear the question, "Isn't the investigative program you are proposing expensive?" We can only reply that each client must consider the alternatives, one of which may be great losses in the business' productivity and profitability. We understand just how expensive it is to carry out an investigation. A relatively low incidence of recognized intentional acts makes complex security programs and costly investigations difficult to justify. Nevertheless, a safe, drug-free workplace is essential to profitability.

Too often, we see extremes in our business. Many clients are complacent and take the attitude, "It can't happen here." Others approach their problems with an attitude best described as paranoid. Neither perspective is realistic. Complacency can lead to serious trouble; paranoia can lead to overkill. Some problems can be ignored and will go away, given sufficient time. Criminality and drug abuse, unfortunately, don't seem to fall into this category. Alternatively, it doesn't take much imagination to engage in overkill. Anyone can turn a college campus or hospital into a modern-day Stalag 17. What most clients need is to have their problems professionally identified and analyzed by investigators who can then design an investigation that meets the unique requirements of the client. It becomes relatively easy for both parties to agree on cost-effective solutions to the company's problems.

When considering the question of how much security in the workplace is enough, one cannot help but recall the words of the famous author, Herbert Spencer: "There is a principle which is a bar against all information, which is proof against all arguments, and which cannot fail to keep a man in everlasting ignorance—that principle is contempt prior to investigation.''

Good security is not cheap. Of course, the cost of an investigation (to the degree it can be forecast) should not exceed the cost of the problem. But in business, one cannot pay a little and get a lot. When a business deals with the lowest bidder, it is well to add something extra for the risk one must take. And, if one does that, one will have enough to pay for something better.

## Investigative Disclosures

Information developed as a result of the undercover operation and the interview process should be treated with the same regard as any other information contained in the files of the client's personnel department. In order to avoid charges of defamation of character, the intentional infliction of emotional distress, and invasion of privacy, all information generated by, in, and during the investigative process must be classified as confidential and handled accordingly.

When the informed assistance of additional management personnel becomes necessary to the investigation, these people should be brought into the process on a very selective basis. Legal counsel, public relations, and labor relations employees are some of the people who may have to be involved in the investigation toward its conclusion. The investigator must ensure that everyone has a complete understanding of the importance of confidentiality. He or she cannot assume that everyone knows how to handle sensitive information. It is wise to take the time to conduct a briefing on the consequences of disclosing such information.

## Indemnification

Different investigators and their clients have different policies regarding whether or not they indemnify one another against litigation. Practically, both the practitioner and the client should realize that any investigation into employee malfeasance carries the risk of litigation. For the client, the best protection against needless litigation is to hire a professional investigator with the skills to avoid basic mistakes. For the practitioner, it is important to warn the client that the investigation could be needlessly exposed to scrutiny if the client makes desperate decisions regarding the administration of discipline at the end of the investigation. If these precautions are taken and both the client and the practitioner are properly insured, mutual indemnification is usually unnecessary.

## POTENTIAL IMPACT ON EMPLOYEE MORALE

An investigation of the type discussed in this book cannot help but have an impact on employee morale. How the investigation is conducted will determine whether that impact is positive or negative.

Most people have a well-developed sense of right and wrong. If the investigative process is seen as being fair and impartial, most employees will understand the necessity for the company's action. On the other hand, if management assumes that everyone in the work force is a potential suspect and reacts to the problem with overkill, most fair-minded employees will be affected adversely. We have seen ample evidence of poorly conducted investigations to support this conclusion.

In chapter 8 we discuss the role of the human relations consultant. Among other things, he or she assesses the investigation's impact on employee morale and makes recommendations on how management can deal promptly and effectively with any related problems.

When major problems of theft and drug abuse exist in the workplace, most employees who are not involved (usually, the majority) express a sense of overwhelming relief when management finally gets around to addressing the problem. No one is more sensitive to safety in the work environment than workers who may themselves be exposed to danger because of another's drug use. Likewise, most right-thinking people, when faced with the consequences to themselves of theft in the workplace, are anxious to have the issue resolved quickly and the working environment returned to normal.

## WHY THE EMPLOYER SHOULD NEVER DICTATE THE METHODOLOGY USED

Some well-meaning employers, when initially presented with the five-phase program set forth in this book, have requested part but not all of the program. Our position on this issue is simple: anything less than addressing all the issues in a thorough, professional manner will reduce the effectiveness of the program and greatly increase the risk of litigation. The five-phase program was designed to minimize (or eliminate, if possible) the consequences of civil liability for labor-law violations on the part of both the investigator and the employer. While the program we recommend may at first appear to be a bit expensive, by the conclusion of the investigation it will prove to have been extremely cost-effective.

## LAW-ENFORCEMENT LIAISON

Evidence of drug abuse often surfaces early in the course of most undercover investigations—usually in the form of misuse or sale of illegal substances. As briefly discussed earlier in this chapter, when these activities are discovered, it is necessary for us to advise the client that we can no longer keep the investigation "private." It is illegal in most states for civilians (including private investigators) to buy, use, or possess controlled substances. With the permission of the employer, the investigative agency must establish a liaison with the police in order to become involved in otherwise illegal drug transactions. Generally, the police do not like to spend time and effort assisting an outside agency with private investigations unless it is to their benefit. One way to ensure that it is to their benefit is to enable them to make arrests and sustain a successful prosecution and conviction. Those, after all, are among their primary functions. Police agencies are often judged not by their success in crime prevention, which is difficult to measure, but by the number of arrests and convictions they make.

## Law Enforcement versus Private Drug Investigations: The Paradox

Traditionally, law enforcement agencies have been charged with the investigation of crimes against society, which usually take the form of street crime or white-collar crime. Of course, when a crime is committed on private property (e.g., in a commercial or industrial facility) and the police are called, they will respond and, if appropriate, make an arrest.

But when the police are called on to bring their resources to bear in an investigation of a potential or suspected problem, such as internal theft or the use of illegal drugs on company time and property, they are usually reluctant to participate. The primary reason for this is limited manpower. On more than one occasion, we have been called by employers requesting investigative assistance with internal theft or drug abuse after having been turned down by the local police. One employer faced with a serious problem of internal theft and diversion of company property, upon making a complaint to the local police, was asked, "If you suspect that your employees have stolen, why don't you just fire them?" When the employer replied that proof of theft was necessary in order to make an insurance claim to recover some of the loss, the police official remarked, "We are not in the business of assisting companies in making insurance claims." He went on to suggest that the company hire a private investigator. This proved to be excellent advice. After a successful private investigation, the employer was able to prove the theft and diversion of over a million and a half dollars of product and had enough facts to file a substantial fidelity insurance claim. Three "trusted" employees and a local buyer of the product subsequently pleaded guilty to ten counts of grand theft.

In the absence of overwhelming evidence that a serious problem exists at a given commercial or industrial facility, the police will more often than not decline to become involved in the initial stages of an investigation. This is especially true concerning the use of illegal drugs on company time and property. As it is, local police departments, with limited budgetary resources, are fighting a losing battle against drug-related crime in the public sector—the number-one crime problem in America today. Nevertheless, our experience strongly suggests that many drug pushers have found it to their advantage to come in off the streets to peddle their wares in the relative safety and security of the commercial and industrial environment.

It seems paradoxical that the constituted guardians of public safety often defer to private investigative agencies in the conduct of drug-related investigations. It is possible, however, for investigators to obtain the assistance of law-enforcement agencies in investigations of substance abuse in the workplace.

## Selling the Program to Law-Enforcement Agencies

### Be Sure You Fully Understand the Law

A private investigator who wants to request the support of local or federal police authorities must be able to demonstrate a full understanding of the applicable laws on controlled substances. If the police officials with whom the investigator is attempting to establish liaison get the impression that he or she is an amateur, they will more than likely refuse to cooperate.

One of the best ways to convince the police of one's credentials as a competent, professional investigator is to talk to them in terms they understand. It is not sufficient to have a theoretical knowledge of the laws on controlled substances, although that is a good starting point. It is necessary to have a day-to-day practical knowledge of the evidence required to prove the commission and elements of a crime (the corpus delicti) in a particular jurisdiction.

Federal authorities are generally not interested in a case unless there is evidence of a substantial illegal movement of controlled substances, particularly in interstate commerce. Local dealers and users, regardless of where they ply their trade, are generally of little concern to federal agents, who usually prefer that local law-enforcement authorities handle such problems.

### Explain the Community Benefits

It helps if the investigator can explain how a particular private investigation can be beneficial to the community at large. This is probably easier to do in substance-abuse cases than it is in internal theft cases. Internal theft is generally confined to the workplace, whereas substance abuse has its roots and tentacles in the community.

### Leave the Decision to Prosecute to the Police

Arrest, prosecution, and conviction are the bread and butter of most police agencies. It will help the private investigator to better plan a police-assisted investigation if he or she understands this. In drug-related workplace investigations, the trend seems to be not to prosecute casual users. Most are either allowed to continue in their jobs under probationary agreements or to resign. The prosecution of sellers, however, varies according to jurisdiction.

Prosecutors have difficulty in taking legal action against casual drug users because the evidence needed for conviction has usually been consumed. It is also impossible to prosecute an alleged seller when no one has actually bought an illegal substance from that person and submitted it to a qualified laboratory for examination. Prosecution is thus usually limited to persons from whom an investigator or police officer has purchased an illegal substance in a manner that meets with the approval of the local prosecutor.

It is a sign of the times that in many urban areas, prosecutors are simply unable to prosecute all drug offenses. Many of them cannot keep up with all the major drug deals, much less the sales of small amounts. As a result, prosecutors often prioritize their prosecutions according to their perception of the seriousness of the offense. Drug offenses in the workplace are often at the bottom of a prosecutor's "seriousness scale" because of the relatively small amounts of illegal substances used and sold. It is not uncommon for prosecutors to justify the rejection of a case with such reasoning.

Another common reason for the rejection of workplace drug cases is the prosecutor's lack of familiarity with cases handled by private investigators as agents of the police. If a buy is not actually witnessed by the police (often physically impossible in the workplace), some prosecutors will use this as an excuse for not considering the case for prosecution. We therefore recommend that arrests of employees only be made on the basis of a warrant issued by the local prosecutor after he or she has reviewed the evidence in the case. If the intent of the local prosecutor is not to try the case, the employer and private investigator are then spared the exposure to civil liability for an allegation of false arrest.

The commander of the local narcotics squad is often the person best able to explain the local district attorney's position on violations involving the sale and use of illegal substances. Once the investigator has this information, he or she can better explain to the employer the probable outcome of the investigation in terms of public prosecution. It should be noted that prosecution may also mean news coverage. In our experience, this occurs rarely and only in exceptional cases. Nevertheless, the final decision as to whether or not a given individual will be prosecuted should rest with the local authorities.

Many company officials like to view police action and subsequent prosecution as a convenient way to justify the firing of bad employees. The police, on the other hand, take the opposite view. As one police official we have worked with stated, "We are not here to clean up their garbage; if they have problem employees, they should just fire them." Unfortunately, many police don't realize how difficult it is to fire problem workers without evidence to support the discharge proceedings.

There is a way to bridge the gap between the two viewpoints so both the employer and the local police can accomplish their objectives and meet their responsibilities with regard to the issue of illegal substance abuse or internal theft in the workplace. The following will detail some methods we have used successfully to bring the two parties together on common ground.

## Limiting the Duration of Police Involvement

Once the local police are convinced that the investigation will be conducted in a professional manner, they must be shown that they can reap the benefits of a successful investigation (either directly or indirectly) without expending too much of their precious time, energy, or resources, all of which are needed to keep up with street crime. An investigator with a track record of reliability and dependability can usually accomplish this and enhance his or her chances of gaining police cooperation.

## Get a Commitment of "Buy" Money from the Client

One of the commitments we have found to be successful when we work with the police is to have the employer provide the "buy" money (i.e., to be used to purchase illegal substances). This reduces the paperwork of the police and allows them to devote more time to the operational aspects of the case.

It also underscores the legality of the investigator's purchases of illegal substances. In most jurisdictions, an undercover operative would be committing a felony by purchasing a controlled substance without the authorization and supervision of the police. We know some investigators who will buy illegal drugs when it seems clear that a subject intends to sell them, the rationale being that without the manifestation of that intent, no crime was committed. We strongly recommend against such conduct. Too many things can go wrong, not the least of which is an operative's buying drugs from an undercover police officer.

## Provide References

Probably the most effective way to establish a law-enforcement liaison is with references. Police agencies have a long-established history of mistrust for private investigators in general. Nevertheless, this bias has been overcome by investigators who have proven themselves to be qualified professionals. Having successfully worked with several law-enforcement agencies, an investigator can provide a creditable reference list to other law-enforcement agencies. The list of references will grow as he or she handles additional investigations in various jurisdictions. A word of caution, though: A good reputation is difficult to establish. A bad reputation can be established with just one serious mistake.

# Chapter 6

## Phase II:
# The Undercover Investigation—
# Administrative Guidelines

One of the most used (and often abused) techniques available to investigators is the undercover operation. No other tool in the investigator's kit can get to the core of an internal problem (theft, drugs, industrial espionage) so quickly, thoroughly, and effectively. But if an undercover investigation is to be as effective and productive as possible, the investigator must approach it with a great degree of foresight and planning. Unfortunately, it isn't always easy to mount an effective undercover operation. Part of the problem, admittedly, rests with employers who demand instant action when they discover that trusted employees may be committing acts detrimental to the well-being of the company.

The Five P's hold for undercover operations as for all other investigative techniques: proper planning prevents poor performance. Without the proper amount of advance planning, initiative, and foresight, no investigator can accomplish the desired objective and successfully resolve the client's perceived problems.

## THE UNDERCOVER INVESTIGATION DEFINED

One of the most effective ways to discuss a topic is to first define it. There are a number of definitions for an undercover operation. We like "a deep infiltration or penetration of a defined objective, using an acceptable cover, to gather information or evidence."

Most undercover operations in the workplace have one of three purposes. Although we will discuss each separately, they are in fact closely interrelated. They are:

- Intelligence—Gathering information of a general or specific nature.
- Discharge—Gathering information and evidence to support termination proceedings.
- Prosecution—Gathering evidence to support a criminal prosecution.

One of the earliest recorded examples of a successful undercover operation for the purpose of gathering intelligence is found in the biblical story of the Battle of Jericho. Joshua sent two spies into the city of Jericho to infiltrate the enemy encampment. Upon returning to friendly lines, the spies reported on the enemy troops' dispositions, supplies, and morale. The outcome of that battle is still celebrated today in a well-known spiritual ("Joshua fought the Battle of Jericho / and the walls came tumbling down").

Modern examples include those of undercover work done by Matt Cevetic and Herb Philbrick (the latter wrote, "I led three lives"). Both were undercover operatives who had infiltrated the upper levels of the U.S. Communist party to gather intelligence data for the Federal Bureau of Investigation (FBI). These investigations occurred prior to the prosecution of the leaders of the U.S. Communist party for violations of the Smith Act in the 1950s. The case officers controlling the operations of Cevetic and Philbrick did not give much thought to the rules of evidence or the Fourth Amendment's prohibition of illegal search and seizure. In a pure intelligence-gathering operation, legally admissible evidence is of secondary importance if it is of any importance at all. Indeed, the legality issue is often totally ignored. The primary objective is to gather intelligence information for its own sake and for subsequent use in the planning of counter-action (*disinformation* is the current term) against the opposition. More often than not, the data so gathered is never divulged, at least not publicly.

The much-publicized ABSCAM operation was a classic example of a different kind of undercover operation successfully conducted by the FBI. It was designed to gather legally admissible evidence for the prosecution of certain public officials, all of whom were successfully convicted. All the convictions were upheld on appeal.

All undercover intelligence operations, whether political or military, follow the same general guidelines. First, the objective or target is identified by the responsible agency. One or more agents are then assigned to infiltrate the objective or target and report on specific issues. On the basis of the undercover agent's report, the case officer (control) recommends the action to be taken to solve the problem. The recommendation is usually intended to eliminate, neutralize, or control the problem.

The intricacies of undercover operations conducted in business and industry seldom take on the complexity of political and military investigations. Nevertheless, the principles for planning remain the same.

## RECRUITMENT AND SELECTION OF OPERATIVES

### Characteristics of a Good Undercover Operative

Above all else, an undercover operative must have a genuinely likable personality. He or she should be a successful salesperson type—someone who sincerely likes people and relates well with others, and is naturally extroverted and gregarious. No amount of acting skill can make up for a lack of these characteristics. It is also helpful if the operative is physically attractive, because people are naturally drawn to attractiveness.

Operatives must possess good to excellent communication skills. They will use these skills constantly in writing and dictating reports. When operatives are called on to testify in court or at an administrative hearing, they must be able to explain their activities.

In our experience, it has been difficult to find otherwise suitable candidates who can speak and write intelligently. Written communication skills are especially hard to come by. Writing is almost a dying art. It is easier to find an investigator with the skills of a Sherlock Holmes than it is to find someone who can write a decent report.

Finally, good operatives must be able to work with a minimum of supervision. They must be self-starters and be capable of exercising good judgment under stress. What we would really like to recruit is a combination of John Wayne and Oliver Wendell Holmes. A difficult set of requirements, you say? Of course it is! Nevertheless, candidates who possess some but not all of the aforementioned skills and traits can often be trained to be very effective operatives.

Some candidates, especially at first view, appear to have all the necessary traits and some of the requisite skills to become successful operatives, but for some reason they never become comfortable functioning in covert situations. The chief task of the case manager is to quickly determine which candidates are performing successfully and which are not. In covert situations, especially for the case managers, there is no substitute for experience.

## Selection Techniques

Undercover operations require the performance of unique and demanding activities under stressful and often dangerous conditions, and not every investigator is adaptable to this type of assignment. The truly excellent undercover operative is indeed a very special breed of person. The quality and success of an operation is, however, in large part determined by the methods and standards employed by the investigative agency in recruiting operatives—one of management's most difficult and time-consuming tasks. We have found that a combination of several recruitment techniques is often the most fruitful approach. We have used all the techniques described below with varying degrees of success.

*Newspaper Ads.*   A "blind" ad is one that does not identify the name of the recruiting agency and requests that written responses to the ad be mailed to a post-office box. This is an excellent and fairly inexpensive method of recruiting. It has the advantage of allowing the agency to screen out potential problems and obtain some quality résumés while remaining anonymous. We use and recommend this as an initial recruitment technique.

*Other Investigative Agencies.*   Some agencies do not maintain a full contingent of undercover operatives, because their needs are seasonal. These investigative agencies cannot keep their undercover operatives employed year-round. If a cooperative spirit can be developed among friendly competing agencies, information concerning the availability of experienced operatives can often be communicated within this closed circuit. This system works well for undercover operatives who work as independents and has the advantage of keeping quality operatives fully employed. A word of caution though: in many states independents must be licensed as private investigators. Many agencies hire unlicensed independents in an effort to save employment costs, unwittingly rendering the investigations they conduct illegal. This could be the cause of serious legal problems, or at the very least a major embarrassment.

*Law-Enforcement Agencies.*   Contacts with various law enforcement agencies may yield information concerning individuals who are readily adaptable to undercover operations. Often the individuals recommended have worked as sources or informants for a law-enforcement agency and thus come equipped with some of the knowledge necessary to be a successful undercover operative. Some may even have specialized training in drug-investigation techniques, with a proven track record of accomplishment in this area. Be leery of criminal "snitches" whose credibility is often self-evident.

*Criminal Justice Programs.*   We have had some success in hiring college students who are enrolled in, or have graduated from, a criminal justice program. Having a contact on the faculty of such a program who can act as a spotter for potential undercover operatives can be very helpful. Students can be extremely productive in positions that they can hold part-time (e.g., fast-food worker, security guard) while completing their schooling.

*Personal Friends.*   Personal friends of agency management, especially those with law-enforcement or security backgrounds, can be an effective source of potential candidates. These contacts, who understand the investigative business and its unique requirements, can effectively screen potential candidates and recommend only those who seem capable of functioning effectively in an investigative environment.

*The Targeted Company.*   As a last resort, the investigative agency could consider using an employee from within the work force of the targeted company. Admittedly, this recruitment source carries a real risk. Nevertheless, when properly trained and supervised, a carefully selected person from within a company—even one with no prior investigative experience—can be a very effective source of information on a continuing basis. One distinct advantage of this type of recruitment is that the operation can begin almost immediately, as there is no need for the usual adjustment period required for a newly recruited operative. Obviously, information obtained from an informant employee must be used carefully so as never to divulge that worker's participation and thus jeopardize his or her continued employment.

As a general rule—especially in regard to sensitive or possibly dangerous operations, such as one in which the problem is the suspected use and/or sale of illegal drugs—an investigative agency should use only experienced undercover operatives. To do otherwise is to play Russian roulette with both the operation and the safety of the undercover operative. The agency must never lose sight of the fact that when faced with the prospect of exposure, disgrace, and prosecution, some malefactors can be dangerous.

## Background Investigation

Some authorities in the field insist that all potential undercover operatives should be subjected to a polygraph examination before being hired and trained. Some agencies require operatives to successfully complete an additional polygraph examination after the conclusion of one investigation before they are assigned to another. This technique is common among intelligence agencies that employ operatives overseas or in unsupervised environments. It helps ensure that operatives remain honest (at least to their employer). It can also help eliminate embarrassing surprises for the agency, especially if a case leads to a trial in which the operative must testify. The enactment of the previously mentioned, restrictive polygraph legislation has severely limited this approach.

As an absolute minimum, any potential undercover operative should be subjected to routine credit, criminal, past employment, and reference checks and pre-employment drug screening before he or she is allowed to undertake any assignment on behalf of an investigative agency.

## Further Pre-employment Screening

Clearly, not everyone who would like to be an undercover operative is suited to the task. We recommend the following techniques for screening otherwise acceptable candidates.

First, place a blind ad in the help-wanted section of a local newspaper. In part, the ad should read: "Experience as an undercover operative is not necessary. Interested applicants must respond in writing, furnishing a résumé or statement of prior education, background, and experience." For expediency, a special telephone number used only for the purpose of screening can be listed. (See Appendix J, "Telephone Application Form.")

After a critical review of the written responses, the agency sends letters to selected individuals, inviting them to a one-day free seminar conducted at a local hotel. Breakfast (rolls, juice, and coffee) is served. The morning session of the seminar is devoted to a lecture (about three hours in length) in which the basics of undercover investigation are presented to the attendees. We have had between fifty and one hundred attendees at such sessions.

After the lecture, the attendees who are still interested are asked to take a written comprehension test based on the information presented in the lecture. The candidates who successfully pass the test are asked to return at 1:00 p.m. for further screening. The remainder are thanked for their interest and excused from further participation.

At the afternoon session the remaining candidates are asked to fill out employment applications, are afforded personal interviews, and are further screened as to suitability for undercover operative training.

The applicants who pass this stage are then asked to appear at the offices of the investigative agency for additional interviewing and screening. The applicants are advised that a further condition of employment and continued employment may be a paper-and-pencil honesty test, a thorough background investigation, and preemployment drug testing. Those who refuse to waive their right to privacy as a precondition of the background investigation are given no further consideration.

Each employment application is then thoroughly reviewed, and all pertinent information contained in the application is verified by background investigation. Selected candidates who are still up for consideration after these checks are invited to join the firm at a trainee status, usually for up to 2 years, depending on their past experience. Upon successful completion of the training period, the trainees become journeyman members of the investigative agency.

Out of one hundred candidates, an agency can usually expect less than ten solid applicants to survive this rigid recruitment and selection process. The ones who do survive, however, usually go on to become excellent undercover operatives and eventually investigation supervisors.

## TRAINING

In our opinion, the training (if any) given to many undercover operatives is poor at best. In some instances, "training" consists of a briefing on the suspected problem and on-the-job training during the course of the assignment. Fortunately, agencies that rely solely on this approach self-destruct in rapid fashion. On the other hand, those that use it with investigators who have some previous formal training or education can often be successful. This should only be done, however, with the full knowledge and consent of the client, so that everyone starts out with a full understanding of the operative's limitations.

It is incumbent upon an agency to use only well-trained personnel on investigative assignments. To get well-trained personnel, however, takes time and patience. Newly hired operatives should always be "broken in" with less demanding assignments than those given to seasoned operatives so that they have a chance to learn (more on this in the upcoming section entitled "Training Assignments").

### Case Studies

Trainees should be given selected case studies of prior investigations completed by the agency (both successful and unsuccessful) for review. This will help them gain a thorough understanding of the agency's procedures and techniques for conducting undercover operations and will familiarize them with proper report-writing procedures.

## Specialized Training in Drug-Related Investigation

The majority of the undercover cases handled today deal at least in part with substance abuse in the workplace and related issues. Education in the subject of substance abuse is an essential part of undercover training. Numerous textbooks on the subject are available, and cooperative members of local law-enforcement vice squads, doctors, pharmacists, and toxicologists (preferably with a track record in the identification and treatment of alcohol and drug abuse problems) are often willing to give training lectures. Additionally, many coordinators of employee assistance programs have experience in behavioral observation and awareness training and make excellent teachers.

Experienced undercover operatives and case managers from the agency's own staff can also provide excellent training on the practical approach to the investigation of drug abuse in the workplace. We set up periodic seminars at which operatives meet with experienced staff members to discuss the experiences and problems they encounter in the field.

## Rules of Evidence

Training in the identification, marking, and custody of physical evidence is beneficial. As a minimum, operatives must have a clear understanding of the "Fruit of the Poisonous Tree Doctrine" as it relates to the admissibility of evidence in both judicial and administrative hearings. Additional subjects, such as coercion, the legal rules for obtaining both written and oral evidence, the differences between legal and illegal searches and seizures, and entrapment should all be part of the basic training program for operatives. For example: If an illegal search occurs (the tree) the evidence obtained as a result of that search (the fruit) is not admissible in evidence against a subject in a criminal trial.

## Entrapment

It might be well at this juncture to point out a common misunderstanding regarding the subject of entrapment. Entrapment is not a crime. It is not listed as a criminal offense in any of the state criminal codes with which the authors are acquainted, nor was it listed in Title 18 of the United States Code as a criminal offense the last time we researched the subject. Entrapment is, however, a defense against a crime, and a rather unique defense at that. When using entrapment as a defense against a criminal act, one is admitting that he or she did commit the crime charged.

In criminal cases, entrapment can be engaged in only by a law-enforcement entity or its agent (e.g., an authorized and properly supervised private investigator), not a private citizen. Private investigators should be aware that entrapment is often used effectively as a defense by unions and plaintiff's attorneys in arbitrations and civil lawsuits because it goes to the heart of the issue of fairness. Therefore, proper case management dictates the avoidance of entrapment. The following definition of entrapment, taken from the draft study of the proposed Federal Criminal Code, Section 702(2), may be used as a yardstick:

> Entrapment occurs when a law-enforcement agent induces the commission of an offense, using persuasion or other means likely to cause normally law-abiding persons to commit the offense. Conduct merely affording a person an opportunity to commit an offense does not constitute entrapment.

Section 702(3) of the same draft study defines law-enforcement agent as follows:

> Includes personnel of state and local law-enforcement agencies, as well as the United States and any person cooperating with such an agency or acting in expectation of reward, pecuniary or otherwise, for aiding law enforcement.

Under case law, the person entrapped is the person whose predisposition to be entrapped is controlling. In other words, if an investigation establishes that an employee has engaged in a given act before the investigation started, it can then be effectively argued that entrapment is not an issue because the employee already had a propensity to commit the violation. Similarly, the prior record of a hardened criminal can be used as evidence against his or her claim of innocence. One way our investigators establish whether a suspected drug dealer has sold drugs before is to make a buy contingent on the dealer's providing the names of references who can attest that the drugs are of good quality.

## Training Assignments

A trained but inexperienced operative can gain much-needed experience through an on-the-job training (OJT) program. In such programs, the novice operative is assigned to a job that involves no specific allegations of wrongdoing to gather what we call general intelligence information. This presupposes a cooperative client—perhaps a manager of a chain of fast-food operations or hotels—who is willing to allow the agency to furnish a novice operative for the mutual advantage of OJT and the general intelligence the assignment may generate. If substance abuse or theft is discovered by the novice, then a more seasoned investigator can be assigned to the case in place of or in addition to the trainee.

Private agencies typically have been tempted to downplay their new investigator's lack of experience in the hope of availing them of some field experience. We have had great success in assigning novices to work for clients who are willing to hire an inexperienced investigator because they have a need for intelligence but a low budget for investigations. A truly symbiotic relationship can develop between a novice investigator and such a client if the costs are kept substantially lower for the use of an inexperienced investigator.

## Investigation of Internal Theft

Controls working in most commercial and industrial environments generally find that progress is slow in investigations of internal theft. This, coupled with the fact that few culprits will steal in a crowd or in front of a stranger, necessitates that we teach our operatives to be patient. Patience and the ability of the operative to become accepted as a peer by the employees are the elements essential to the success of an undercover operation.

Operatives should also be taught not to underestimate the significance of a single case of petty theft or drug use. What an operative observes could be the proverbial tip of the iceberg. A trained interviewer may find that a simple incidence of petty theft is the lead that will enable him or her to uncover a complicated internal theft ring. It is generally (though by no means always) true that employee theft is not a one-time offense. Once employees learn it is easy to get away with stealing small items, some will go on to steal bigger and better things.

## Limiting False Information

Some agencies have had problems with undercover operatives who manufacture false information as a means of staying in the good graces of the case manager and, of course, extending their assignments and thus remaining on the payroll. We suggest controlling this tendency in several ways.

First, all potential operatives should be thoroughly tested, investigated, and screened for honesty prior to being considered for hire. Once hired, they should be permanent employees of the agency. All operatives should be made to understand that the information they gather will be used by an interview team and verified during the interview process, which is explained later in this book. Finally, operatives should understand that more than one undercover investigator may be used on each assignment. They will rarely know who the other operative is or when he or she may be assigned to the case. The mere knowledge of this helps to keep an agency's operatives honest.

## Feigned versus Actual Drug Use

On occasion, undercover investigators are faced with the temptation to use drugs to solidify their cover. In supervising covert operations involving drug buys, most law-enforcement agencies will not countenance the use of drugs by private undercover investigators or even their own sworn police officers. The only exception would be if an investigator were likely to be in physical danger if he or she did not use the drugs. For such situations, undercover operatives, whether private investigators or police officers, should be trained to feign the use of drugs. If properly documented, feigned use can later be an effective defense against allegations that the investigator committed an illegal act, or accusations of entrapment. If not properly documented, feigned use can impeach the credibility of an investigation.

Feigning drug use is acceptable during an undercover investigation if it is necessary to convince drug-abusing employees that the operative is a user as well as a buyer. Unfortunately, it is not easy to feign the use of most drugs (a good example is cocaine). Marijuana use can, however, be successfully feigned, inasmuch as an investigator can hold the end of a cigarette and pretend to inhale without actually doing so. This method is best left to experienced investigators, who are usually good actors. Attempts to convince employees that an investigator is a drug user might have the opposite effect if the "actor" does not give a realistic performance.

We only allow an investigator to pretend to use marijuana and limit that permission on the basis of the investigator's experience and the circumstances of a given investigation. The best course of action is for undercover investigators to develop covers in which they admit that they used to use drugs but do not anymore. This allows investigators to purchase drugs (ostensibly for a friend) while having an excellent explanation as to why they themselves do not use drugs. It is also a good practice to toxicology test all feigning incidents to ensure there has not been any actual ingestion of the drug feigned.


## OPERATIVE EMPLACEMENT

### The Uncontrolled Entry

Of the several methods of inserting an undercover operative into the workplace, the uncontrolled ("cold") entry method is by far the safest and usually the most productive. Its disadvantage is that it is the most time-consuming approach.

In this method, the operative appears at the personnel office of the targeted facility and asks for a job application, with the hope there will be a vacant position. No one in the company, including the client, need know the operative's true identity. An obvious problem with this approach is that there may never be an opening for which the operative is qualified. Or it may take weeks, or months, to gain a cold entry into the targeted facility. Meanwhile, the problem that is the basis for initiating the undercover investigation may continue unabated. In such instances, the agency can arrange for the client to create a new position, and the operative, armed with the ideal credentials, can apply for the job before anyone else. If sufficient time is devoted to the process by the client and the case manager, the operative can be briefed as to the personality, likes, and dislikes of the individual who will interview him or her for the job. The primary duty of the operative is to become the "perfect" applicant who arrives to apply for the position at just the right time. If properly briefed, the operative should be able to rise above any other applicants, who will have far less insight into how to obtain the position.

The average employer is often too impatient at the initial stage of the investigation to wait for an operative to use this method of entry. The investigative agency needs to explain to the employer the favorable cost/benefit ratio of this appoach.

## The Controlled Entry

In the controlled entry method, someone in a decision-making capacity, usually the employer, makes arrangements for the operative to submit an application for a specific job at a specific time. The operative is then hired immediately by the manager or the personnel office. This hiring technique is more common than one might imagine. It is often done under the guise of "doing a friend a favor," but that pretense should only be used as a last resort. A new employee who may be thought of as a conduit of information to management may come under intense scrutiny from other members of the work force. This could preclude the operative from being accepted in the workplace.

When the controlled entry is used, the fewer people who know the true identity and mission of the operative, the better. Under no circumstance should anyone's secretary or assistant be made aware of the existence or identity of the undercover operative. Many people lead dull lives. Few can be trusted not to share confidential tidbits with their office friends over lunch or coffee. This is not to suggest that only secretaries or assistants gossip. It is to suggest that not even the long-time secretary of an informed manager should know about the undercover operation. He or she may not deliberately sabotage an operation, but even a slight disclosure can necessitate ending an investigation abruptly. One way to guarantee an undercover operation's failure is to allow it to become common knowledge among the employees of the target facility. More cases are prematurely terminated for this reason than for any other.

## Unusual Circumstances, Proven Techniques

It is always the agency's responsibility to devise, in cooperation with the employer, the strategy necessary to place the operative in the position that will best enable him or her to accomplish the mission. With a little thought and some imagination, even the most difficult of challenges can be overcome. Union considerations notwithstanding, it may be feasible to create a temporary position in which to place the operative. An expansion of the work force in a particular department can usually be justified. Most supervisors complain that they do not have enough manpower to accomplish their goals.

We have arranged for the creation of summer or between-semester internship programs for college students in order to place operatives into data-processing environments. And janitorial positions—which usually allow for total access, even into research and development departments—can be used as a last resort.

It may be necessary to place the operative in any department of the facility where vacancies exist until he or she can be transferred to the department (or shift) in which the problem is suspected to exist. In a multiplant environment, the operative's cover can be that he or she has been transferred from a plant in another geographical location.

A former client can be an excellent source of documentation of past employment. Documentation is especially important for operatives who have difficulty meeting the employment requirements of a facility. We once had an assignment to place an operative in a specialty meat-packing and mail-order house. It was essential that the operative have a basic understanding of the meat-packing process. With the aid of a former client in the packing industry, we were able not only to train the operative but to document him as having been an employee of a meat-packing processor in another part of the country.

In situations where the company has been laying off workers, or simply is not hiring, we have found the following approach to be effective. One of the executives of the company tells those who are unaware of the investigation but are responsible for hiring the operative that a local training organization (representing a government program such as CETA) has met with company officials. The executive can claim that the company has committed itself to hiring one of the program participants. It can be explained that the company will benefit by having an employee for half the cost of a regular employee, since the program will pick up the other half of the employee's pay. The hiring can also be passed off as the company's civic responsibility. The investigators can have a special telephone line set up in their office so that if anyone from the company calls for verification, the telephone will be answered with the name of the program.

Another approach that has worked well for us in larger companies has been to create a new "pilot management-training program." In this program, executives tell the supervisors who are responsible for hiring that even though the company is laying off workers, they have decided to establish new manager-trainee positions that will allow trainees to work in various non-supervisory positions throughout the company, not only in different departments but at different facilities. The rationale behind the program is that future managers will manage better if they have experienced the positions that they will later be asked to supervise. We have used this pretext even in unionized companies that were laying off workers. Of course, being a manager-trainee can carry with it the stigma of being a conduit to management. We have found that investigators with gregarious personalities have been able to shed this stigma quickly.

## The Employment Application

The employer should furnish the case manager with several blank copies of the firm's employment application. Case managers should assist the undercover operative in filling out the application so they can both agree on the basics of the cover story. Once the application is completed, the operative can appear at the employment office, obtain another application, and either fill it out on the spot, using the agreed-upon cover, or ask to return the application later. In either event, potential inconsistencies in the operative's cover story are eliminated before the application is submitted.

At this point in the investigation the employer should be reminded that the longer it takes to successfully place an operative in the target facility, the longer it will take for the operative to become a productive agent. Once the operative is in the work environment, one can usually expect a period of adjustment of four to eight weeks. The operative needs this much time to establish the relationships that will allow him or her to effectively gather information concerning employee wrongdoing.

## Limiting Knowledge of the Operation

During the basic training program, operatives are taught that the one element essential to the success of an undercover investigation is the cover story. Every effort must be taken to ensure that the operative's cover remains functional, not only during the active phase of the investigation but (for reasons discussed later) long after that phase ends. Operatives are taught that for their own safety and security they must never reveal their true identity to anyone at the target facility, under any circumstances. Operatives must understand that if they do so, they may be subject to immediate termination.

The client must be similarly instructed. We can think of no exception to this basic rule. In fact, it is much preferred to terminate the undercover operation than to reveal the cover of the investigator prematurely. The reason for this is obvious. One can always reestablish a fully concealed undercover investigation at a later date. Once a cover is revealed, however, an employer's chance of reinstituting an undercover operation in the same work environment becomes extremely poor.

To protect their cover, operatives should obtain unlisted telephone numbers at the very least. Many metropolitan areas have phone systems that will allow a "dead line" in the agency office to be forwarded to an investigator's home, should that operative need an untraceable phone number. This is especially important when it is impractical for an investigator to move to a new residence at the end of every case.

To date, we have not had a case in which an operative's Social Security number has been traced to a home address, but this is clearly possible. To fabricate a Social Security number will surely cause an operative major headaches in the future. One must weigh the risks of each situation and then be guided by those risks. One possible solution, when practical, is to have the operative register an untraceable address with the Social Security Administration. Realistically, however, the tracing of Social Security and Internal Revenue information is difficult enough for experienced investigators and is probably beyond the abilities of those who are being investigated.

Some agencies have a "hold harmless clause" in their investigative contracts, specifying that if the employer or any employer representative is responsible for revealing the existence of an undercover investigation, the agency cannot be held responsible for the consequences. In fact, the employer is held fully liable for the safety and security of the operatives involved. We have found such clauses are most often unenforceable.


## Handling Unusual Expenses

We encourage our operatives to engage in company social activities, such as softball games and picnics, as a means of solidifying their position within a group of employees and gathering as much information as possible in a variety of settings. The operative should be reimbursed for any associated expenses, which are then passed on to the employer.

There may be other expenses as well, such as relocation costs if the operative has to move from a distant locale. Such expenses as travel, mileage, telephone, uniforms, union dues, and money spent at the local bar or pizza parlor entertaining co-workers are also reimbursable by the employer. Not to encourage and be willing to reimburse the operative for these kinds of activities and expenses may well prolong the amount of time it takes to successfully resolve the case.

## Paying the Operative

Undercover operatives work at two jobs and are thus entitled to receive two wages. In addition to working, for example, on a warehouse loading dock for eight hours a day, forty hours a week, operatives must constantly perform their primary functions as investigators.

For a job such as warehouse worker, the operative should be on the regular company payroll and receive a weekly paycheck, just like any other company employee. In addition, the operative is entitled to be paid by his or her parent investigative agency an agreed-upon fee to cover investigative activities. This fee should include any overtime that the operative may work in pursuit of his or her assignment.

Often this aspect of double pay must be explained to employers who do not understand why they must pay the operative for a full forty-hour work week and then pay the agency additional monies for the operative's undercover activities. Once they hear the explanation, most employers understand the logic of the arrangement and have no difficulty with payment procedures.

## OPERATIVE SUPERVISION

Those outside the investigative industry tend to believe that undercover investigations in the workplace are very dangerous—probably because of Hollywood fiction. For the most part, undercover investigations by private security agencies are far safer than those conducted by police narcotic units. The subjects of workplace investigations are usually well known and relatively stable members of the community. Of course, this is not to say that conducting these operations is the safest profession known to man. All undercover investigations should be approached with the knowledge that there is a real element of danger, even though it may not be as big as that in some investigations in the public sector.

Because of the potential for danger, the first consideration in any investigation should be the safety of the undercover investigator. If there is any doubt about his or her safety, it is always better to err on the side of conservativeness. There is no better reason to have experienced supervisors oversee investigations.

In order to maintain control as well as discipline, the case manager must insist on daily written reports from all operatives. The manager also should receive at least one telephone call per day from the operative. More frequent contact is necessary if the case is complex or has reached a critical point, such as an imminent theft from a warehouse, the hijacking of a truck, or a major drug buy. More frequent contact may also be necessary if the operative is relatively inexperienced or if the nature of the case is such that constant supervision is an essential element of the operative's safety.

We believe that the daily written report is essential because it allows the case manager to be no more than twelve hours away from the events reported. This gives the case manager the opportunity to offer guidance to the operative and to brief the client. It also allows the case manager to edit reports to smooth out any inconsistencies, should they exist, before forwarding a completed case report to the client. Daily written reports also tend to give the case a disciplined structure and make the agency's records more professional.

## Techniques of Supervision and Control

The case manager should meet personally with the operative as frequently as necessary to ensure that the investigation proceeds along the lines previously agreed to by the agency and employer. Meetings should always be in an out-of-the-way place, in a controlled environment, where the chances of being observed are reduced to an absolute minimum. We suggest a restaurant or motel room (in sensitive cases) located in a part of town away from where the operative works or lives.

Operatives should ensure that they are not followed when they report to a meeting with the case manager. There are several ways to accomplish this. One is never to go directly from work or residence to the prearranged meeting place but rather to proceed by a circuitous route. Another is to resolve all doubts by placing a call to cancel the meeting rather than taking the chance of being observed making contact with the case manager. In this regard, one should never underestimate the intelligence or the resources of one's opponent. Complacency on the part of an operative can be his or her greatest enemy. Effective operatives remain alert and sensitive to their surroundings at all times.

## Establishment of Emergency Communications

The principals should develop and agree upon a system of emergency communication at the outset of the operation. The ability of the operative to communicate with the case manager and the case manager to communicate with the client must be firmly established before a problem arises. An emergency that requires such communication may never occur. Once it does, however, it is almost always too late to set up an effective procedure to deal with the emergency. The key is to plan ahead.

An agency that employs full-time undercover operatives (and all should) ought to have such procedures developed as a part of their standard operations. That way their operatives will always have the ability, regardless of the day or the hour (most emergencies occur after normal work hours or on weekends), to contact their supervisors when the need presents itself. Likewise, the agency should always be able to reach the client in an emergency, day or night.

## Use of More than One Undercover Operative

As mentioned earlier, it is sometimes advantageous to use more than one undercover operative on the same assignment. Factors that may dictate multiple operatives are the following: the size of the population within the target facility; the suspected scope and range of the problem; the complexity of the investigation; the dangerous nature of the investigation; the need to verify and validate reported data.

It is unnecessary for an operative to know the identity or the existence of other operatives on the same assignment. Where exceptions are made to this basic rule, sufficient justification must be set forth in writing, and the final decision must be made by someone with authority over the case manager. The client should always be made aware of the exception.

We would like to think all our operatives have been properly selected and adequately trained so their every action will reflect favorably upon the agency. Real life does not always work this way. Any time multiple operatives are assigned to a case, one should be a seasoned, mature veteran with the proven ability to function in a covert assignment with a minimum of supervision. The case manager can then feel comfortable knowing, should anything out of the ordinary occur, that he or she can call upon the resources of an experienced operative at the target facility—one who can be depended on to exercise proper judgment and take the necessary action while keeping the operation on track.

Too often, for the sole purpose of increasing billings to their clients, some private investigators sell multiple undercover operatives. If the methodology outlined in this text is used, even in facilities with several hundred employees, seldom will it become necessary to use more than one experienced, well-placed, and well-supervised operative.

## OPERATIVE AND CLIENT REPORTS

During the initial phase of a case, the agency should establish an agreement with the client regarding the submission of reports. Such details as to whom the reports should be sent, to what address (never to the client's office), how often they will be sent, and what kind of information they will contain should all be part of the discussion.

To avoid compromising the operation, we recommend that all written correspondence, including case reports, be sent to the client's home address or, in cases of maximum security, to an established post office box. Reports sent to the client's office, regardless of how disguised, will sooner or later fall into the hands of an inquisitive mail clerk or secretary. If that should occur, one must consider the entire operation compromised. The best approach is simply not to allow this to happen. We also recommend to clients who receive reports at home that they not carry them to the office in their briefcases. The entire file should remain at home or at a safe location away from the office.

## Dissemination of Reports to the Client

An effective procedure, and one that should be worked out in advance with the client, is not to have written reports distributed for the first three or four weeks of an active investigation. The operative will, of course, still write a report for each day of activity. These will be accumulated by the case manager and held until the first face-to-face meeting between client, case manager, and operative (see the upcoming section entitled "The Monthly Debriefing").

Significant problems uncovered during the initial phase of the investigation can be handled by the case manager and the client by telephone. We have found that some employers become too emotional when they first receive written confirmation that their worst fears were true. The idea that trusted employees may have been involved in activities adverse to the best interests of the company is difficult for many employers to accept. When faced with absolute proof that such things as theft, industrial espionage, or drug-related crimes have occurred, some employers have been known to become quite upset. Some have openly confronted the employees being actively investigated and on whom the operative is just beginning to accumulate evidence, thus bringing the investigation to an untimely demise. Situations such as this are best avoided by giving the employer the information in a controlled environment. The employer can then be allowed to vent his anger and frustration without jeopardizing the operation.

## Preparation of the Case Summary

We suggest that reports from operatives cover five basic categories: Dishonesty, Physical Security, Employee Malfeasance, Supervisory Inefficiencies, and Employee Attitude toward Management. Naturally, this list can be expanded as needed. Both positive and negative aspects of the employer's operations are reported on daily by the operative. All original reports from operatives should be maintained in the permanent case file at the agency.

After fifteen to twenty working days' worth of reports have accumulated, the case manager can separate out the incidents reported and prepare a summary of the data received, using the five categories listed above. This summary, which we call an impact report, is a narrative of the major events that have occurred and have been reported during the fifteen- to twenty-day period. The most important information is presented at the beginning of the report, and the least important at the end. Related events are grouped. If an employee has made drug sales on several occasions during the reporting period, for example, these incidents are grouped in chronological order so the client can more easily see the full impact of the employee's transgressions. Grouping related events in this manner is much more effective than mixing them in with all the other events in the report.

This approach has also been found to be more effective than furnishing employers with copies of the operative's daily reports. Most employers are not interested in the daily blow-by-blow details of an investigation. The impact report eliminates most such details and focuses mainly on the objective of the investigation.

## The Daily Report from the Operative

Receiving timely reports enables the case manager to deal with information on a current basis. The daily report should be a "same-day" report. That is why we recommend a system that allows operatives to dictate their reports over the telephone. This is preferable to a system based on mailed reports, which may take several days to travel from the operative to the office. The key element to the whole aspect of the daily report is it lends structure and supervision to an otherwise unstructured and difficult to supervise type of investigation.

Once finished with the day's activities at the target facility, the investigator should immediately prepare a written report according to a structured reporting outline. He or she should then dictate the contents of the report by telephone to a central dictating unit located at the agency office. Units are available that allow one to dictate, review, and edit by using the buttons on a touch-tone telephone. When the operative completes the call, a central processing unit inside the dictating machine attaches a data strip to the dictation tape that tells the transcriber the date, time, name of the operative, and case number.

Of course, not all agencies have this sophisticated equipment. Without it, however, operatives must either bring their reports to the agency or mail them on a daily basis. We have found that the deficiencies in both these methods more than justify the expense of this kind of equipment, especially for an agency determined to supervise each case closely and provide its clients with timely information.

We suggest that an agency transcribe reports from operatives the same day they are received. This way the reports are available to the case manager for review the next working day. The advantages of using such a procedure are obvious.

There are, of course, other methods of communication, some more professional than others. Too often what we have seen is the occasional telephone call between operative and case manager after the close of business, from which the manager may write a report that is then submitted to the client. This procedure may work for a while. It will not, however, stand the test of time, an administrative hearing, or a judicial review of the investigation, in our opinion. Quite simply, it changes second-hand information into third-hand. As such, it is not the original report of the investigator who gathered the information, and its probative value may therefore be questionable.

## The Monthly Debriefing

Once a month, the case manager, client, and operative should meet at a discreet location to discuss the progress of the case. We recommend that notes of this meeting be taken and a written report be kept in the permanent case file. The discussion should cover what has happened in the past month, the current status of the case, and the direction the investigation is expected to take in the immediate future.

It is important that everyone at the meeting fully understand and agree on these three aspects of the investigation. Any disagreement should be resolved at the meeting. In the absence of full agreement as to the future direction of the investigation, especially on the part of the client, we recommend that the investigation be suspended until the difference is resolved.

## The Incentive Award Program

All good organizations reward employees who produce results. Both the agency and the employer enjoy the benefits of effective work by an operative. We recommend a program that rewards operatives by sharing profits, based on the following elements of productivity:

1.  Successful completion of the assignment.
2.  Timely submission of all written reports.
3.  Quality and quantity of information received.
4.  Successful meeting of the client's objectives.
5.  Willingness to follow supervisor's instructions.

The incentive award, in the form of a bonus, is paid by the agency out of its profits from the case. The bonus is paid to the operative only after completion of the assignment. This bonus is not a bounty to be paid on the basis of a "body count" of drug dealers or thieves. Rather, it is a reward paid at the end of the case for a job well done.

This technique, recommended by the authors, has measurably improved the overall quality of the information-gathering process and has markedly decreased the problem of assignment abandonment. The longer an assignment lasts, the more incentive there is for the operative to maintain high investigative standards. One would like to think that most operatives would perform well regardless of financial reward. Proper recruitment, selection, and training can go a long way toward minimizing problems. We believe that an incentive award program adds icing to the cake, builds morale, and improves professionalism among an agency's operatives.

# Chapter 7

# Phase III:
# The Confrontation

## STING OPERATIONS (PURCHASES OF
## DRUGS OR STOLEN PROPERTY)

A planned confrontation may begin with a "sting operation." In such an operation, one undercover agent introduces implicated employees to another (often, more experienced) undercover operative. The second operative can be introduced as either a "fence" for stolen property, a drug dealer, or both, if applicable. When the introduction is made, the second operative questions the implicated employees as to their methods and motivations, as well as how long they have engaged in the illegal actions. People tend to respond freely to such questions when they have been conditioned to believe that the fence is someone they should try to impress. This can be accomplished if the first operative suggests that his or her contact is able to increase the profits from thefts or drug sales while reducing the risks. Subjects of a theft- or drug-related investigation often respond to the question "What makes you think you can get away with this without getting caught?" in the way one might expect a job applicant to answer a question about his or her employment qualifications. The answer will often include not only how they get away with it but also how long they have been doing it and with whom. Furthermore, these employees are usually willing, with a little coaxing, to furnish information that implicates others in the work force who are involved in the same or similar activities. Those who have been working at the facility for a long time can provide much more information than the operative could possibly learn during the course of the investigation. In fact, the undercover operation should yield about 10 percent of the information ultimately collected in each case, and the interview process should provide the remaining 90 percent.

Once this information is collected, the investigative format changes. The implicated employees are allowed to repeat the violations as often as necessary to enable the undercover operatives to catch them red-handed. Once caught and faced with the proof of their guilt, such employees generally admit their wrongdoing.

This technique is a classic example of "roping," as opposed to entrapment, in which a police officer (or agent) causes someone to commit an illegal act that would not otherwise have been committed. When properly interviewed, culpable employees will usually admit that they were engaged in a given violation prior to the inception of the investigation, thus negating the issue of entrapment.

## THE INTERVIEW PROCESS

The interview coordinator supplied by the investigative agency is the glue that holds the interview team and the entire interview process together. Arrangements for office space and all the equipment (e.g., recorders) necessary for the interview process are made by the interview coordinator. The coordinator also keeps a log, documenting the time of each interview, and is responsible for relaying all the new information gained from one interviewee to the persons responsible for interviewing other implicated individuals. In this manner the investigators are constantly updated. The coordinator is also responsible for collecting and filing all written and tape-recorded confessions, as well as the notes (if any) taken during each interview.

### Preparing the Interview Matrix

Once the sting operation has been completed, the interview coordinator should prepare a structured interview format. This is one of the most crucial activities in an investigation, and one that demands a great degree of expertise.

Using all previous reports on the investigation, the coordinator compiles an interview matrix (summary sheet). The interview matrix should contain all the pertinent information on each implicated employee and be cross-referenced according to the type of malfeasance (e.g., theft, drug sale, drug use). Additional information needed by the interviewer, such as background data obtained through credit, criminal, and Department of Motor Vehicles checks and personality profiles, are obtained from the employer and the operative and added to the interview summary workbook. This background information is vital when interviewing implicated and suspected employees.

### Composition of the Interview Team

Only seasoned investigators with a track record of being quality interviewers and interrogators should be on this team. These investigators must have a complete understanding of the labor-law issues associated with the interview process. Apprentice or trainee interviewers do not have the necessary qualifications. As mentioned earlier, the exposure to allegations of false imprisonment and wrongful discharge are greatest at this stage of the investigation.

It also helps if the interviewers have experience in investigating the illegal sale and use of drugs, as well as internal theft. Persons who are addicted to alcohol and drugs often develop a defense mechanism known as denial, which must be fully understood if one is to be successful in interviewing them.

We have found that former law-enforcement officers with vice-squad experience are often well suited to interviewing after they receive training in labor law. As discussed earlier, most police officers are not familiar with labor-law issues and need this training. It should also be noted that the goals of law-enforcement interviews and interrogations are not as complex as those of interviews conducted in the workplace.

## EXPLAINING THE INTERVIEW PROCEDURE TO THE IMPLICATED EMPLOYEE

At the beginning of the interview, and before any questions are asked, the employee should be advised as to what to expect during the interview process. The interviewer should make every effort to help the employee relax and listen carefully to this explanation.

The employee should be told that the employer has been concerned for some time about certain problems affecting the company's ability to make a profit. If illegal drug use is an issue, the interviewer should state that the employer has a responsibility to provide a safe and secure work environment for its employees, and that illegal drug use can seriously affect the employees' safety, as well as the company's ability to produce a quality product—which in turn affect its ability to remain competitive in the marketplace and to ensure the continuing employment of its work force. The interviewer may also wish to briefly discuss such things as fidelity insurance, work-related accidents, worker compensation, and the correlation between quality control and profitability.

The interviewer should tell the employee that the company hired the investigative agency to gather information concerning these problems. Now that a substantial amount of information has been collected, it is necessary to resolve these issues in a fair and impartial manner.

Some investigators suggest providing details to the interviewee concerning some of the investigative techniques that were used to gather information. This is often done in an effort to disguise or downplay the contributions made by undercover operatives, who may still be working at the facility in some final phase of the investigation. The interviewer should never suggest that any illegal or questionable technique was used. For example, in a state where the use of electronic surveillance without a court order is regarded as an invasion of privacy (this is the case in most states), the interviewee should not be told that this technique was used. This information could be used as the basis for lawsuits against both the company and the investigator for invading the employee's privacy in order to gather incriminating evidence against him or her.

## THE ESSENTIALS OF THE SIGNED STATEMENT

Once an interviewed employee has orally confessed to any transgression, a written signed statement is taken. The employee is asked to include the following essential elements in this statement:

1. Acknowledgment that he or she has been offered representation (if appropriate).
2. Acknowledgment that he or she has been told the interviewer is a private investigator hired by the employer, not a police officer.
3. Acknowledgment that the statement was given freely and voluntarily and was not induced by threats or promises on the part of the interviewer.
4. A detailed list of the offenses he or she has verbally admitted to the investigator, how many times those violations were committed over how long a period, the first and last times the violations occurred, and the dollar amounts involved in cases of theft or drug deals. This statement *must* specify that the violations occurred on company time and/or property.
5. Details on the involvement of other employees who have committed like offenses.
6. An account of his or her motivation for engaging in the confessed actions.
7. An explanation of why he or she willingly confessed, knowing that the result could be termination, prosecution, or both.
8. A statement indicating what he or she would consider as appropriate disciplinary action for the offenses admitted.

For additional information, please refer to Appendix F (Written Declaration Checklist).

## INTERVIEWING WITHOUT ALERTING THE ENTIRE WORK FORCE

When the supervisor of an investigative interview team first discusses the interview process with company managers, it is important to determine how to interview the implicated employees off the work floor without alerting the entire work force that an investigation is underway. If the company's personnel manager would ordinarily go onto to the work floor to escort an employee to the personnel office only in the event of a disciplinary meeting, he or she would be ill-advised to do so during the investigative interview process. The reason for this, of course, is that if employees who have been buying from a drug dealer were to see the dealer being escorted to an interview, they might quickly surmise that it is because of the drug selling and might therefore make commitments to one another not to admit their involvement, should they be called in to an interview. On the other hand, if they are completely unaware that an investigation is underway, at least for several hours, the investigators might have an opportunity to gather enough information to get well into a second or third wave of interviews before knowledge of the investigation becomes commonplace among the work force.

One effective way of getting the first group of employees to their interviews is to have a management representative request, through normal channels, that these employees come to a particular area of the facility. This should be accomplished without lying to any middle-level supervisors about the purpose of such a request. Most high-ranking managers do not need to explain themselves to middle managers and can simply say that they need some help. A manager can then intercept each of these employees on their way to the assigned location at a place where few employees will see the diversion. With a little careful planning, most of the culpable employees can be brought in for their interviews before any of the others have a chance to discover what is going on and get their stories straight.

## THE ROLE OF THE EMPLOYER REPRESENTATIVE ON THE TEAM

One or more employer representatives, usually from the personnel department, should be assigned to the interview team. They will benefit by obtaining a full understanding of the interview and interrogation process. Also, in addition to bringing employees into the interview room, they can fill several important purposes at various stages of the interview process:

1. They can witness that all employees are treated fairly and with courtesy and dignity by the other members of the interview team.
2. They will be present in the room with the employees and interviewers when the employees read their signed statements aloud, thus ensuring no coercion was used to obtain the confession.
3. Employer representatives will ultimately determine what disposition will be taken regarding the culpable employees and advise them of same. They can also answer any questions the employees may have regarding their future with the company (which should purposely be left unanswered until the investigation is concluded).

## THE TAPE-RECORDED STATEMENT (ORAL DECLARATION)

The tape recorder should be used only after the employee has voluntarily furnished a written signed statement and while the employer representative is in the interview room. At this point, the interviewer may take the tape recorder out of a briefcase and place it on the table.

It is extremely important to gain the subject's cooperation in the use of the tape recorder. This is accomplished by explaining to the employee that although the signed statement gives the interviewer a clear picture of his or her side of the story, the employer representative now needs to hear the employee read the statement, for several reasons. For one thing, the issues are complex, and it will save time for the employee representative—the decision maker—to hear the story directly from the employee, not second-hand from the interviewer.

The interviewer then commences to dictate into the tape recorder, setting the stage for what is to follow. What has just been accomplished is this: the subject has acccepted the fact that a recording is being made without the interviewer having asked him or her for permission to record the session. Taped evidence obtained in this fashion will usually meet the legal requirements for admissibility (i.e., all parties to a conversation being recorded must know that a recording is being made). Although in some states a tape recording is admissible as long as one party to the conversation is aware that it is being made, we think it is only fair that all parties to the conversation be told. Knowledge is the issue, not permission.

Once employees have confessed verbally and in writing, they rarely object to having their statements recorded. If an employee does object, the investigator should tell the employee that he or she is free to choose not to speak. The recording can then proceed, with the interviewer explaining the details of the case to the employee representative; the employee only needs to object if the interviewer's explanation is incorrect. The interviewer can then read the employee's signed statement. In the absence of an overt objection by the employee to the details of the signed statement, the investigator merely asks the employee one question: "Is this your statement, and is it true and voluntary?" If the employee answers orally, his or her response will be recorded. If the employee merely nods, the interviewer can state this fact into the recorder. Either method can be used to prove that the statement is true and was given freely and voluntarily, without the investigator using either threats or promises to obtain it.

During the final stage of the tape recording, the interviewer should once again establish, in the presence of the employer representative, that the employee has been treated fairly, and that no coercion, threats, or promises were used by the interviewer to obtain the confession and the subsequent signed statement. The simple way to accomplish this is to ask the pertinent questions of the employee in a manner that evokes a narrative response rather than a yes-or-no answer.

The employer representative should be coached to express the company's gratitude for the employee's cooperation after the interviewee has admitted wrongdoing under oath and with the tape recorder on. The employer representative should also express concern and disappointment regarding the malfeasance and inform the employee that a final decision regarding his or her future with the company will be made in the next few days, after all the information from the investigation has been obtained and reviewed.

There are decided advantages to tape recording a confession with the tacit approval of the subject:

1.  The recording will clearly indicate the voluntary and spontaneous nature of the confession and its authenticity.
2.  It will establish the noncoercive atmosphere in the interview room and will help to verify that the interviewer dealt fairly and justly with the interviewee—points that may be disputed if only a written confession is obtained.
3.  It will be evidence of the questions asked and the interviewing techniques used, so that the employee cannot allege that the interview was handled otherwise.
4.  Much can be inferred about the integrity of the process by listening to the recorded narrative responses and the tones of the participant's voices.

The aforementioned interview procedures will not absolutely guarantee that a dispute will not surface at a later date in the form of an employee grievance, arbitration, unemployment hearing, or civil litigation. But if used as set forth, these procedures will substantially reduce the chances of this happening. If a dispute does occur, these procedures will help ensure that both the employer and the interviewers are in a favorable position to successfully defend themselves against allegations of wrongdoing.

## THE ROLE OF THE MANAGEMENT CONSULTANT

Upon completion of the investigation and interviews, one of two effects is generally observable among the workers who remain employed:

1. The majority are pleased that management had finally decided to doing something about the problem, OR
2. The majority harbor a noticeable hostility toward management for taking disciplinary action against some employees for something management let get out of hand in the first place.

It is important that management be prepared for either reaction. After all, one of the objectives of initiating an undercover investigation is to increase the client's productivity and thus profits, while minimizing the loss of assets. It therefore makes economic sense for a company to be concerned about the attitude of its functional employees. In certain environments, an investigation can be the catalyst for a union-organizing attempt.

It is also important to identify why the malfeasant employees committed the acts that resulted in their being subjected to disciplinary action. Armed with insight into what caused the wrongful acts, the employer will be better prepared to enact measures that will create a better environment for the company's present and future employees—an environment in which employees will experience less temptation.

To address these vital issues, we recommend that our clients seek the services of a management consultant. This expert can make recommendations beyond the scope of loss prevention by truly analyzing the human dynamics of the employment environment. Although many companies share common problems, analysis often shows that the underlying reasons for those problems are unique to each individual firm.

The management consultant should be introduced to the client during Phase I of the investigation to review the company's present policies and help formulate the approach to be taken. The consultant should also join the interview team at its initial briefing and be given an opportunity to become aware of all aspects of the case by reading the summary reports of the investigation furnished to the client by the case manager.

Immediately after each interview, the management consultant should meet with the interviewed employee in a private session. The purpose of this meeting is to determine:

1. What kind of employee the subject was when he or she first began working at the firm.
2. The employee's motivations for committing the wrongful act(s).
3. What the client might have done to improve or eliminate the circumstances that led to the employee's temptation and subsequent malfeasance.
4. Whether the employee would like to address any comments to management on other issues.

The management consultant's interview with the employee usually produces two results. First, it establishes that the company is sincerely interested in improving working conditions. This helps to eliminate or reduce the hostility that is often expressed by the work force at this stage of the program. Second, it serves to identify problems such as the absence or inadequacy of screening, training, and supervision, which often increase the odds that employees will engage in wrongdoing.

## INTERVIEWING TECHNIQUES OF PROVEN SUCCESS

It is important to differentiate between employees proven to have actually been involved in conduct that could cause their termination, suspension, or prosecution, and employees who have simply been implicated by others. Obviously, interviews with employees who have been proven to be involved in improper conduct will be more intense. Interviews with employees who have only been alleged to be involved in improper conduct will be less structured, giving the employees an opportunity to explain any conduct that gave rise to the allegation.

Regardless of the type of interview conducted, it is essential for the interviewer to establish the nature of his or her relationship with the interviewee at the outset. We have found the following techniques helpful in accomplishing this:

1.  Let the interviewee know he or she will be treated in a fair and impartial manner. Make it clear that the interviewer, not being in a supervisory or managerial position with the company, is not in a position to promise the employee that he or she will not be fired or prosecuted in return for an admission of guilt, a signed statement, or cooperation. The interviewer is only a gatherer of facts, not a decision maker.
2.  State that the best the interviewer can do is give the employer the employee's statements of the facts. No further inducement should be made.
3.  Both the written and recorded statements by the employee should be taken as declarations. A declaration is an oath under penalty of perjury. This will discredit the subject of an investigation who, subsequent to giving a confession, recants or contends that he or she was somehow coerced into confessing.

Witnesses at all judicial and most administrative hearings testify under oath. If an employee contends at such a hearing, under oath, that his or her prior statements were not an accurate account of what transpired during the investigative interview, the obvious question is, which oath is to be believed—the oath administered at the time the statement was taken, both orally and in writing, or the oath administered at the hearing? (Frankly, it doesn't matter when the individual commits perjury. Since both statements are sworn to be true, one of them has to be false.)

In such a situation, the subject's credibility is impeached rather than the interviewer's. This has a way of dramatically shifting the burden of proof if the judicial or administrative inquiry does in fact continue beyond this point.

Please refer to the written and oral declaration checklists (Appendixes F and G). Investigators should take care to ensure that all the items on the checklists are included in the employee's declarations. They include not only statements on what the employee did, how long he or she did it, and who else was involved in the wrongful activity, but also statements that address all the tortious allegations we have ever known to be used to impeach the credibility of a confession made to an investigator in a similar interview. If all these issues are addressed during the interview, the employee will not only admit his or her guilt but also will clearly state that the interviewer did nothing improper in conducting the interview. You will notice that in the Written Declaration Checklist, only the introductory words for each statement are shown. We advise interviewers to allow the employee to complete the sentences in his or her own words. You will also notice that a catch-all statement is also included near the end of the checklist, to allow the employee to add anything to the statement in his or her own words. This helps to preclude the allegation, often made by plaintiff's attorneys, that the investigator put words into the mouth of the accused employee. Likewise, during the tape-recorded oral declaration, the investigator should not ask questions that can be answered with either yes or no, but questions that prompt a narrative response. Following these guidelines will greatly reduce the likelihood that an attorney will prevail in an attempt to discredit the employee's statement.

## THE CONTROLLED STANDBY: REASONS AND EXPLANATION

In order to avoid creating problems having to do with "desperate treatment" (see chapter 4, "Legal Considerations"), the employer must review all the information available after the interview phase of the investigation has been completed before making any decision regarding discharge, discipline, or probation. Whatever course of action is taken, it must be done in a fair and impartial manner. To do anything less will not withstand the scrutiny of an administrative or judicial inquiry.

We recommend that the client representative place the employee in a temporary "controlled standby" status, with full pay pending further investigation, and send the employee home. This procedure serves several purposes:

1. It enables the interviewer to truthfully tell other employees who are interviewed that no one who was interviewed before them has been fired or disciplined in any manner.
2. It prepares the client to enter the next phase of the program, which deals with establishing criteria for the fair and equitable administration of disciplinary action.
3. It relieves some of the pressure on employees being interviewed, who may in turn be less likely to withhold information for fear they will be fired, regardless of whether they cooperate or not.

# Chapter 8

## Phase IV: Discharge or Retention of Employees

The client should be assisted, usually with the advice of its labor law counsel, in establishing criteria for the administration of disciplinary action (reprimand, suspension, termination, and possibly prosecution). Across-the-board criteria for dispensing discipline put principles above personalities and help decrease the risk of litigation alleging discrimination in the form of disparate treatment.

In terms of discipline, disparate treatment is dispensing one form of punishment to one employee or class of employees (e.g., supervisors) and another, usually more severe, punishment to another employee or class of employees for the same or a similar offense.

We recommend a meeting of the following persons to discuss disciplinary action:

1. The interview team and case manager.
2. The employer representatives, including the personnel officer who was part of the interview team and as many of the decision makers as possible.
3. The employer's labor law counsel.
4. The management consultant.
5. A qualified toxicologist.

The interview team manager should chair the meeting and should bring to it copies of all signed statements, the tape-recorded interviews, and the investigative case file. Everyone present should be prepared to discuss recommendations on discipline for the various levels of misconduct discovered during the investigation. The interview coordinator can assist by distinguishing those employees whom the evidence has clearly established as ringleaders, thieves, and drug dealers from those found to be less culpable.

### COOPERATIVE VERSUS UNCOOPERATIVE EMPLOYEES

Experience shows that while the vast majority of employees, when treated fairly, will cooperate in the final phase of the interviews, some will not. There are various reasons for employees' intransigence when interviewed. However, the reasons are of little importance. Employees who refuse to cooperate even when faced with evidence sufficient to support discharge proceedings should be considered for immediate termination.

Employers will find that there is a great temptation to fire employees who have admitted their guilt. But an employer who is reluctant to fire employees who deny their guilt when the preponderance of proof clearly supports it sets a very bad precedent. The message to the work force is that an employee confronted with malfeasance who admits guilt is fired, but the employer is reluctant to take the same action against an employee who is guilty and professes innocence. Employees who have received this message will simply deny the allegations made against them.

Guilty employees who are not ringleaders or drug dealers and who have exhibited sincere remorse through cooperative and truthful testimony could be considered for continued employment, possibly on probation. If not, employers can at least show compassion by allowing these employees to resign, as opposed to firing them. Always remember that federal EEOC and other regulations may govern the administration of discipline in any given situation.

## BUYERS VERSUS SELLERS

In our opinion, the sellers of illegal drugs are guiltier than the buyers because sellers exploit human weakness for monetary gain, with absolutely no regard for the consequences. The fact that drug dealers are taking time from their primary occupations should be a prime consideration, as well as the effect of illegal drug-related activity on the morale of the noninvolved members of the workforce. Experience has shown that while these employees look kindly upon management's leniency in disciplining less culpable employees, the reverse is true when it comes to drug dealers. For those who sell drugs in the workplace, the greater the risk, the greater the reward—and the greater the punishment when caught. By no means, however, does this mean we believe that users should go undisciplined. In fact, in many environments the best way to "send a shot across the bow" of the workforce often means employers must terminate *all* violators of the company drug policy.

## THE MANAGEMENT CONSULTANT'S
## INDEPENDENT REPORT

With the information obtained from the confrontational interviews and the data extracted from the operative's reports on the case, the management consultant can submit to management a report that outlines what the employees who were caught feel could be changed in the company environment to reduce the chance of the problem recurring.

An attitude survey questionnaire can also be prepared for the employer. This will focus on the major problems experienced at the facility. We recommend waiting for some time (perhaps one to two weeks, but no longer) after the last disciplinary action is taken against an employee, to allow the dust to settle. The consultant should then spend one or two days administering the attitude survey questionnaire to small groups of selected employees. From this survey, two important issues can be determined:

1. The sentiments of the majority of remaining employees after the investigation.
2. What the company should do, in the employees' opinion, to prevent the problems from recurring.

If the attitude of the work force is generally negative, the consultant may help by explaining to employees the importance of the problem to the company as a whole. This should help the majority of employees to understand that their economic livelihood is tied inseparably to a healthy, profitable company, and that most of the issues that came to the surface during the investigation affected safety, productivity, profitability, and therefore the solvency of the company. One would hope that most of the work force would then be able to see the direct benefit to them of the company's actions. At the very least, this process lets employees vent hostility. As a direct result, a return to normal business routines is more quickly accomplished.

The opinions and suggestions of the work force regarding the problem become the subject of the management consultant's independent report. This report can be invaluable to the employer in improving overall conditions.

## WRONGFUL DISCHARGE SUIT CONSIDERATIONS

As stated in chapter 4 ("Legal Considerations"), it is during phases III (confrontation) and IV (discharge or retention) that the greatest legal risk for both the client and the agency is the wrongful discharge suit. Because investigators are not conversant with the day-to-day changes in labor law, a qualified labor lawyer with extensive labor-relations experience should be available to consult with the team at this time.

## REPLACEMENT OF DISCHARGED EMPLOYEES

Once dishonest employees have been removed, new employees will have to be hired to fill the resultant vacancies. By this time, the employer should realize the absolute necessity of initiating proper techniques for recruiting and selecting employees to avoid duplicating past hiring problems. As was pointed out in the Preface, without establishing selection criteria, the client could easily hire as replacements that 20 percent of the labor market that statistically shows a high propensity for dishonesty.

We suggest that the employer institute a self-administered management training program that introduces improved screening, training, and supervisory techniques to those members of the staff who are responsible for recruiting, selecting, hiring, and training new employees. This will be further discussed in chapter 9 ("Phase V: Preventing the Problem from Recurring").

## DRUG TESTING AND EMPLOYEE PROBATION

There is probably no more controversial issue affecting civil rights today than the issue of drug testing. Although most thinking individuals recognize that the manufacture, distribution, sale, use, and possession of illegal drugs must somehow be curtailed, few have any workable solutions to this problem.

Regardless of the issue, be it drug testing or testing for AIDS, when the word *mandatory* is coupled with the word *testing,* hackles are raised. It seems society will choose to ignore such problems as long as they are largely confined to narrow segments of society (drugs in the ghetto, AIDS among homosexuals). However, when the problem affects all segments of society and is seen as being out of control, well-meaning individuals will embrace any solution presented, giving little or no thought to the long-range consequences.

Mandatory drug testing has recently been ruled unconstitutional as both an invasion of privacy and a violation of civil rights. As mentioned earlier, one of the first drug-test cases of national significance was *The Player's Association* v. *The National Football League* (NFL). The Player's Association (a union) took the position that the league did not have the right to force mandatory testing on all players. The NFL took the opposite position and lost. In recent years the league's testing program has, of course, been modified.

In March 1986 in the Superior Court of California, a Stanford student named Simone Levant sued the National Collegiate Athletic Association (NCAA) over the issue of mandatory drug testing for athletes. Ms. Levant, a collegiate diver, objected to being forced to provide urine samples to be tested for the presence of over three thousand drugs as a precondition to competition. She won the case. For most people, the objection to drug testing seems to be, "If we let you indiscriminately take our bodily fluids, regardless of your noble intentions, what's next?" We predict the end is near for mandatory or random drug testing without due cause, unless there is an overwhelming public safety issue.

Fitness-for-duty criteria apply to areas of employment with direct impact on public health and safety. In *Rushton* v. *Nebraska Public Power District et al.* (1987), with regard to the issue of mandatory annual drug testing (for-cause and pre-employment testing were not at issue), the U.S. District Court for the District of Nebraska ruled that there was a compelling interest in assuring the safe operation of the nuclear facility and that "the addition of the Fitness For Duty (FFD) program further[ed] the ongoing process of securing public safety." The judge stated, "I find that compulsory participation in drug testing is the least restrictive means of assuring the continued safe operation of Cooper Nuclear Station."

There are alternatives, but how long they will be permitted is anyone's guess. One alternative is voluntary drug testing as part of a conditional employment agreement.

We recommend this alternative in cases where otherwise functional employees have, by their own admission, used illegal drugs on company time and property.

The conditional employment agreement allows employees who have admitted to using illegal substances on company time and/or property to continue their employment if they contractually agree to submit to random urinalysis. The testing gives the worker an opportunity to prove to the employer that he or she is no longer using drugs, not even on personal time. Failure to take or pass such a test is grounds for immediate termination. Employees who do not believe that they can meet the stringent requirements of this agreement because of addiction should be allowed to volunteer for an employee assistance program. We do not believe it is wise to require employees to participate in rehabilitation programs unless *they* believe they have a problem that they cannot overcome without help.

Random testing of this type would quickly be attacked by civil libertarians if it were to be applied to the work force across the board. We have not yet experienced any difficulty with clients' initiating the conditional employment agreement for employees who have been caught and have admitted their transgressions. The employee can exercise the right to refuse to submit to a test at any time. Then the company is faced with the decision of whether or not to fire the employee. If termination is chosen, then it is for violation of the conditional employment agreement, which was previously agreed to by the employee in writing.

So far this technique has proven to be acceptable to personnel experts, labor lawyers, and consultants. It has one advantage not seen in other programs: it focuses on the problem individual while leaving other employees (nonusers) to continue their lives without being subjected to random fitness-for-duty screening. As far as we know, this procedure has worked very successfully.

# Chapter 9

# Phase V: Preventing the Problem from Recurring

"An ounce of prevention . . . ," as the old saying goes, is the best way we know to describe proactive versus reactive security programs. As we have tried to show in the preceding chapters, one can, through the use of properly applied legal techniques, investigate any problem affecting the internal controls of an organization. Investigators, loss-prevention consultants, and labor consultants are, however, a costly solution compared with the solution discussed here: the proactive program.

## EFFECTIVE DRUG AND ALCOHOL POLICY AND GUIDELINES

Most organizations have recognized the need to provide a drug-free work environment in the interest of employee health and safety. Not all organizations, however, have developed an effective policy or have prepared guidelines for use by managers and supervisors to effectively carry out a program designed to ensure that the work environment remains drug-free.

To assist employers who have not developed a written policy, we have included a sample drug and alcohol policy statement as Appendix I. This statement or one similarly worded, if it is properly communicated to all levels of the organization, is the first step in a series of steps that must be taken by management to address the problem.

If the workplace is to become (and stay) free from the consequences of the illegal use of drugs by workers, on company time and property, the policy must first be published. It must be legally sound, enforceable, and supported by management. Then it must be well communicated to, and understood by, all employees. Good communication means employees must not only understand what the rules are but why the rules exist. One way to ensure this is to communicate the message to employees by every means available.

## HIRING PROCEDURES, BACKGROUND INVESTIGATIONS, AND TECHNIQUES FOR SCREENING OUT DRUG ABUSERS

Almost all the serious problems encountered by the authors with regard to internal theft or the illegal use of drugs by employees can be traced to one location—the personnel office. It sometimes seems that employers are unaware of the vast body of knowledge concerning the proper approaches to recruiting, selecting, and hiring workers. If they are aware of the principles of good hiring practices, one can only assume—in the absence of evidence to the contrary—that many employers honor them more in the breach than in the observance.

In fairness, many organizations do have sound hiring programs. These programs, coupled with excellent background checks and investigations, enable them to develop an excellent cadre of employees and supervisors. In spite of this, something in the system occasionally breaks down and an employee commits a crime such as embezzlement or industrial espionage. When this happens, top management comes apart at the seams and demands an immediate answer to the question "Why?" Upon investigation it becomes apparent that the hiring procedures, as good as they are, need a little "fine tuning." Unfortunately, in our experience, situations like this are the exception and not the rule. What we see, more often than not, is applications taken at face value, with perhaps a cursory background investigation or none at all. One variation seen is that the application is accepted at face value, the applicant is hired, and a quick background check of past employers and references is made at some later date, after the applicant is already in the work force.

Invariably, when inquiries are made of those in charge of hiring, one hears the excuse that in today's civil rights atmosphere it is next to impossible to apply time-honored pre-employment procedures. In our opinion, this answer is partially valid. There is, however, a screening technique that can be helpful. When coupled with a background check, it can help solve a lot of personnel problems at the earliest stage of the process. The only materials needed are an employment application and a pencil with an eraser.

The technique works as follows: A blank employment application is furnished to the applicant, along with a number two pencil with an eraser. The applicant is told to fill out the application and return it to the personnel officer. When the applicant returns the application, the personnel officer takes the application and leaves the room. While not in the presence of the applicant, the officer makes a photocopy of the application and then returns to the counter with the original application in hand. After glancing at the application, the officer states, "This company is very sensitive on issues concerning the accuracy of employment applications. Please take this application back, look it over, and if you have any corrections or changes you wish to make, do it now. Remember, we conduct a very thorough background check on all applicants. Any inaccuracy on the employment application could be grounds for rejection, or termination should the inaccuracy surface after we hire you."

When the employee takes the original application for review, he or she will make any changes by using the eraser to delete the original entry and then writing the new information in its place. Upon resubmission of the application, the personnel officer merely compares it with the copy made earlier. Changes made by using an eraser and reentering new data will be immediately discernible.

Note that most employment applications contain the caveat, usually printed at the bottom of the first page, that false entries may be grounds for dismissal. A false statement on the original application, even if later changed, is indicative of a serious character defect in the applicant. Simply stated, the applicant does not have a high regard for the truth. People who are emotionally mature usually have a well-developed sense of honesty. They deal with reality and conflict in an emotionally mature manner. Drug and alcohol abusers tend to be emotionally immature. Confronting reality and conflict is too painful for them; thus they opt for the quick fix. We would caution employers to concern themselves only with errors of substance. Errors of form are easy to make in times of stress and should be discounted.

While all liars are not thieves and drug addicts, most thieves and drug addicts are liars. In an employment situation, in which the employer can and should resolve all doubts in his or her favor, why take a chance? The time to deal with such problems is before the applicant becomes an employee, not after. Most moral and legal obligations attach after a person becomes an employee; few occur prior to employment.

Some enlightening data have emerged from one employment situation in which a precondition to employment was the taking of a polygraph (lie-detector) test during the application process. Applicants who successfully passed the initial screening were informed that the next step in the process was a polygraph test—entirely voluntary on their part. Applicants were furnished with a list of twenty-five questions, all of which related to honesty. They were told that only those questions would be asked during the polygraph examination. The applicants were then scheduled to return for the test.

It was later determined that 65 percent of the applicants did not return for the second interview. Of the 35 percent who did, about 15 percent of those tried to beat the test by giving false answers to one or more of the questions. This left a population of 29.75 percent from which the agency hired its work force. While one might expect that such a screening process would guarantee a problem-free work force, such was not the case. Occasionally, a bad apple slips through. Which just goes to show that there are no guarantees, whatever method one uses.

There are several paper-and-pencil integrity tests that have won general acceptance by employers in jurisdictions where the polygraph cannot be used in the pre-employment process. We recommend these to our clients as a relatively inexpensive form of insurance against hiring problem employees. One of the regulatory requirements of the U.S. Nuclear Regulatory Commission (NRC) is that employees and contractors who need to have unescorted access to nuclear power facilities be thoroughly screened before being given such access. One of the ways some power plants accomplish this is through paper-and-pencil integrity testing, coupled with a thorough background investigation. Be sure to check the legality of such tests, as they may vary from state to state.

The following companies provide pre-employment testing services:

1. London House, 1550 Northwest Highway, Park Ridge, IL 60068.
2. The Stanton Corporation, 5701 Executive Center, Charlotte, NC 28229.
3. The Reid Report, John E. Reid & Associates, 250 South Wacker Drive, Chicago, IL 60606.
4. P.A.S.S–III Survey, Personnel Systems Corporation, Oak Brook, IL 60522.

There are, of course, others who provide these services, but these are among some of the most commonly known testers.

## TRAINING ADMINISTRATORS AND SUPERVISORS TO RECOGNIZE DRUG AND ALCOHOL ABUSE

Another program found in areas where safety is a prime consideration (such as transportation agencies, nuclear power plants, and air-traffic control stations) is behavioral observation training for supervisors. This program, coupled with what is known as policy implementation training, has been found to be very helpful in spotting the use and abuse of drugs and alcohol. People who have attended these training programs come away with an awareness and understanding of how to recognize these problems and what can be done to solve them before they become uncontrollable.

This book will not go into a full explanation of any of these programs. Suffice it to say that it is not necessary for an employer to develop a screening system by trial and error; there are programs available, many with impressive track records.

## THE RISK-ANALYSIS SURVEY

Even after a very thorough undercover investigation has been concluded, some serious security-related issues may remain unresolved. The undercover investigation's principal purpose was, after all, to identify problem people and problem areas needing resolution.

Dealing with problem people has been treated exhaustively in the preceding pages of this book. Dealing with problem areas, however, necessitates targeting one's physical risks, some of which may have surfaced during the undercover operation. To do this, we recommend the physical-security or risk-analysis survey. If the facility has a security plan, the survey will determine whether the plan is up-to-date and functional in every respect. If the facility does not have a security plan, the survey will establish the need for one and develop some or all of the necessary security services that may be required. Such a survey can assist the client in developing policies and procedures to do the following:

- Protect against internal and external theft, including embezzlement, fraud, burglary, robbery, industrial espionage, and the theft of trade secrets.
- Develop access-control procedures to protect the facility's perimeter as well as assets located internally.

- Establish lock and key control procedures.
- Design, supervise, and review the installation of antiintrusion detection systems.
- Establish an executive protection program for corporate personnel in the United States and abroad to deal with extortion and kidnapping incidents.
- Provide control over the movement and identification of employees, customers, and visitors on company property.
- Review the selection, training, deployment, and operations of security personnel and guards (proprietary or contract).
- Assist in the establishment of emergency and disaster recovery plans and guidelines.
- Identify the internal resources available for the establishment of an effective security system.
- Develop and present instructional seminars for management, supervisors, and employees in all of the above areas.

This list of procedures is by no means all-inclusive. It does set forth some of the programs and systems most frequently reviewed or developed as the result of a security survey.

## HOW MUCH IS TOO MUCH?

As discussed in the description of phase I of the program, having a well-defined and well-communicated policy is a basic tool of good management. A revealing exercise to put supervisors through at the end of an investigation that discovered many major violations against company policy is to ask those supervisors where they set limits for theft and drug abuse. After all, if they are not in agreement as to where those limits should be, there is a great likelihood that they will tend to enforce the limits at various levels. This exercise would, then, consist of determining which level of discipline, from warning to prosecution, supervisors would apply to a variety of acts.

The best way to start this exercise is to begin with the most egregious offense and then work through four or five lesser offenses. Ask the supervisors whether they would warn, suspend, fire, or prosecute an employee for each act. The likely result is that the supervisors will have different ideas concerning which level of discipline to apply to a given transgression. When the exercise is over, it should be clear that not all of the company's supervisors think the same way, and thus they are unlikely to administer discipline in the same manner. It is the duty of the company to get all supervisors to agree at which points various levels of discipline should be applied. Of course, allowances must be made for the review of circumstances on a case-by-case basis.

## EMPLOYEE ASSISTANCE PROGRAMS

No group in our society is free from the problems of alcohol and drug abuse and addiction. These problems are also found in every job category, regardless of age, education, or ethnic background. Thus, the old concept of termination and replacement no longer solves the problem. There is no guarantee that the replacement for an affected employee will be any less susceptible to these problems.

One solution that has gained widespread acceptance in recent years is the Employee Assistance Program. Such programs are provided by many outside agencies, especially hospitals. In many larger institutions they are provided as an in-house counseling service of the employer. It is the objective of these programs to recognize when otherwise effective employees may need professional assistance with a problem such as alcohol abuse, drug abuse, or emotional difficulties, any of which may be interfering with their ability to perform at work.

For example, one financial institution with which we have worked has a program to deal with the emotional trauma experienced by bank tellers who were present during an armed robbery. The program is administered by an Employee Assistance Coordinator. Flight attendants who have survived an airplane crash also benefit from such a program.

There are many differences among Employee Assistance Programs, but the following characteristics are common to most:

1.  The establishment of a policy and guidelines that set the stage for recognition of the problem.
2.  A willingness to provide professional counseling to help employees.
3.  The identification of rehabilitation facilities where employees can go to have their illnesses treated, usually on company time and expense.
4.  The recognition that the responsibility for recovery is the employee's, as it is with any illness. When earnest attempts to help have failed, the employee must be discharged, in a fair and equitable manner, in the interest of good personnel procedures.

For more information concerning this subject, contact the National Council on Alcoholism, Two Park Avenue, New York, NY 10016. Ask for their pamphlet entitled "Labor-Management Approach to Employee Alcoholism Programs." Many states and counties have local alcoholism councils, from which one can obtain additional information concerning alcohol-abuse and drug-abuse assistance programs.

We tend to be advocates of EAP when it is used properly. Programs structured to encourage employees to come forward to seek help work much better than those that force participation as a condition of continued employment (once an employee is "caught"). The main reason for this is the employee has been inherently encouraged to meet the first requirement for successful rehabilitation—to admit the addiction exists.

# PART III

## Toxicology

# Chapter 10

# Drug Testing in the Workplace

**Raymond C. Kelly, Ph.D. DABFT**[1]

Drug testing of employees and applicants is one of the most effective and widely used means of combating the drug problem in the workplace. Over one-third of the nation's largest corporations have adopted testing under certain circumstances. With the popularity of drug testing by employers has come controversy on the part of employees, labor organizations, and civil libertarians. It thus behooves a company considering a testing program to plan and implement it carefully in order to minimize objections and increase effectiveness. This requires appropriate legal and technical advice at the beginning and as the program develops.

## POLICY QUESTIONS

Drug-testing programs in the workplace should be consistent with the company's overall policy on discipline and its stand on drug use by its employees. Before a firm establishes a drug-testing program of any kind, it is wise to evaluate the existing policy and, if need be, revise it. Important policy issues to consider are:

1. Who will be affected by the testing program? New hires, applicants, employees who are promoted, those returning from layoffs, employees injured on the job, employees who appear to be "under the influence," particular classes of employees, or all employees?
2. What type of testing will be performed? Urine testing, blood testing, or testing of other samples, such as saliva or hair?
3. What actions will be taken on the basis of the test results? For example, when will applicants not be hired: when traces are found of any drug, or only certain drugs?
4. What allowances will be made for the use of prescription and over-the-counter drugs and for passive exposure to marijuana?

---

1. Laboratory and Science Director, Laboratory Specialists Inc., Woodland Hills, California.

5. What specific events will trigger testing?
6. How will positive test results be interpreted? Will the mere presence of a drug be cause for disciplinary action, or will there be an attempt to prove the worker's performance was impaired? If so, what kinds of documentation of impairment will be required? What sort of disciplinary action will be taken?
7. Who will approve the necessary changes in company policy before the drug-testing program is implemented?

## LEGAL ISSUES

Many of the legal issues involved in controlling drug abuse in the workplace are covered in chapter 4 of this book. The legal challenges to drug testing encompass a variety of issues, but only those directly related to testing itself are mentioned here. These fall into five areas:

1. Company-policy justifications for the program.
2. Reliability of sample-collection procedures and chain-of-custody system (i.e., the sequence of individuals authorized to handle the specimen).
3. Accuracy of test results.
4. Interpretation of test results.
5. Defensibility of testing methods and interpretations, and the related issue of the competence of the laboratory personnel conducting the test.

## ROLE OF TESTING IN THE OVERALL PROGRAM

As discussed previously, drug testing is only one weapon for combating drug abuse in the workplace. It is desirable to have the drug-testing policy fully developed and in place before any testing begins. Many employers use education, treatment, or employee assistance programs to limit drug abuse among workers. Sometimes a testing program is started on the heels of an undercover investigation. Such an investigation can be crucial to documenting the scope of the problem and justifying testing approaches to manage it. Once the problem has been effectively rooted out, it must not be allowed to recur, and drug testing of job applicants and current employees is part of prevention.

## BIOLOGICAL RATIONALE FOR TESTING

The basic assumption underlying testing is that a drug and/or its biological products, or metabolites, will remain in the body for a period of time and can be detected in biological samples drawn from the individual. Analyses of several biological specimens can be performed, and each has advantages and disadvantages.

Urinalysis, the most common method of drug screening, can reliably identify drug use in recent hours or days. Urine can be obtained without puncturing the skin, in sufficient quantity to perform several types of tests sequentially, if necessary, and to have enough of the sample left over for storage and later reanalysis (if required). Urine can be screened for a large number of drugs simultaneously. The principal disadvantage of a urine sample is that it is inherently nonquantitative. This means that concentrations of a given drug in urine may bear very little relation to the actions of that drug on the body or to the subject's level of intoxication by that drug. Indeed, the finding of a drug in urine normally cannot establish the time of use, the dose, whether the user is an abuser, or whether he or she is still under the influence of the drug.

Blood is another substance that is used for drug testing and analysis. Obtaining it requires a venipuncture, a somewhat painful and invasive procedure. The small amount of blood (a few milliliters) that can be obtained without damaging the patient sometimes limits the number and kinds of tests that can be performed. Drugs are often more concentrated, and thus easier to detect, in urine. They may be present in blood for only a few hours after use, yet detectable in urine for much longer. But to establish whether someone is drug-impaired on the job, blood testing is often useful. The mere presence of a drug in the blood suggests impairment, and a determination of the drug's concentration, interpreted properly in relation to well-known therapeutic and toxic ranges, may help to establish the fact.

In addition to blood and urine, various other biological samples have been proposed for use in drug testing. Saliva is the one most often suggested, primarily for marijuana testing. The idea behind this is that the active component of marijuana, tetrahydrocannabinol (THC), remains in the mouth and adheres to the mucous membranes for a few hours after a marijuana cigarette is smoked. Thus, it is possible to determine whether the drug was used recently. In principle, the same approach could be used to test for other drugs that are smoked, such as phencyclidine (PCP), cocaine, or nicotine. In practice, difficulties with sample collection and the analysis and interpretation of results make saliva a nonpreferred drug-testing sample. Similar considerations apply to analyzing hair for drugs.

## COLLECTION AND HANDLING OF SAMPLES

Drug testing of workers, whether of applicants or current employees, is a type of forensic toxicology (i.e., performed for the purpose of gathering legal evidence). As such, it must be controlled and documented more extensively than most other types of medical testing. In particular, the procedure for actually obtaining the sample for testing must be closely regulated. This is not necessary in routine medical testing, because the test subject has little incentive to invalidate the test. In drug testing, such a motive definitely exists, and the collection of a proper sample becomes more difficult as a result. Important steps in the collection and handling of drug-testing samples include:

1.  Identify the donor of the specimen through valid identification.

2. Have the subject execute a legal consent form for the test (required in many states).
3. Obtain and record the subject's recent history of drug and alcohol exposure (previous month and previous week, respectively). Include brand names, if known. Forward this information to the testing laboratory.
4. Ensure that the donor has no opportunity to switch or tamper with the specimen during the collection process.
5. Upon collecting the specimen, check its integrity (e.g., for urine, check appearance and temperature to document recency of excretion).
6. In full view of the donor, or with the donor's assistance, seal the sample with a tamper-proof seal. Have the donor sign or initial this seal.
7. Initiate a chain-of-custody document—a written record of each person who handles the specimen.
8. Place the sample containers in a tamper-proof package for conveyance to the laboratory by the quickest means available.

Throughout the process, each specimen must be handled individually to ensure that there is no chance of two specimens being exchanged.

## TESTING METHODS

There are two phases of conducting a laboratory analysis for evidence of drug abuse: screening and confirmation. The screening portion of the analysis requires a method that is sensitive, selective (specific), and efficient, because every sample will be processed according to that technique. Samples that test positive for a drug or drug group are subjected to a confirming analysis. Today the most widely used screening methods are thin-layer chromatography (TLC), radioimmunoassay (RIA), and the enzyme-multiplied immunoassay technique (EMIT). The TLC technique removes drugs from a sample by solvent extraction, concentrates them, and separates and detects them on a thin layer of silica gel on a glass plate. As a general screening technique, TLC has the disadvantages of insensitivity and nonspecificity. The immunoassay methods, RIA and EMIT, are based on the use of antibodies to detect drugs. These techniques are extremely sensitive and specific and are preferred over TLC.

The goal of the second stage of testing, confirmation, is to retest a sample that has screened positive for a drug to verify that the drug is present. This requires the use of a completely different scientific method. The finding of a drug by two totally different methods means that the individual has almost certainly been exposed to that drug. The most commonly used confirmation techniques are gas chromatography, high-performance liquid chromatography, and gas chromatography–mass spectrometry. In all these methods, the unique chemical and physical characteristics of the individual drug (as opposed to those of other drugs or of natural constituents of the sample) are used to detect and separate it. In many cases, the result of the confirmation test is further strengthened by the presence in the sample of characteristic metabolites that are produced when body processes act on the drug in question.

## LABORATORY SELECTION

The choice of the right laboratory can be one of the most critical factors in the success or failure of the drug-testing program. If the laboratory produces incorrect results, uses improper procedures and methods, or cannot defend its findings, the tested employees are treated unfairly and the company is placed at legal risk. The quality and competence of testing laboratories vary widely, as demonstrated by nationwide surveys of laboratory proficiency. In the past, there was little that company representatives, as nontechnical people, could do to distinguish good laboratories from bad. Recently, that situation has begun to change as the National Institute on Drug Abuse (NIDA), a federal agency, has begun to provide direction. Two professional organizations, the College of American Pathologists and the Association for Clinical Chemistry (whose members include most of the people who perform laboratory drug testing), have followed suit with their own programs. Laboratories following the protocols recommended by these groups may be assumed to be providing reliable results.

### Clinical Criteria for Selecting a Drug-Testing Laboratory

*Extent of Services*

1. Are both screening and confirmation tests performed?
2. Which drugs are tested for?
3. What procedures and detection limits are used?

*Proficiency Testing*

1. Is the laboratory subjected to a NIDA-recognized proficiency-testing program?
2. Is an interlaboratory comparison review performed by certifying officials?
3. What corrective actions exist for unacceptable results?

*Quality Control*

1. Does an active and periodic review of all components take place?
2. Does documentation of corrective action exist?
3. Is corrective action reviewed by a certifying scientist?

*Procedure Manual*

1. Does a complete procedure manual exist?
2. Is it available to all personnel?
3. Is it reviewed periodically?
4. Does it contain details of all procedures?
5. Does it contain criteria for unacceptable results?

*Specimen Receiving, Preparation, and Storage*

1. What is the chain of custody?

2. What are the methods of ensuring the security of specimens?
3. What aliquoting procedures are used?
4. What are the storage conditions?

## Reporting

1. What are the criteria for written reports?
2. What are the criteria for telephone reports?

## Reagents, Controls, and Standards

1. Do proper labeling and documentation of reagent and chemical standards, purity, and identity exist?
2. Are proper numbers of blind and open controls used?

## Instruments and Equipment

1. What analytic instruments and equipment are available?
2. What are the instrument maintenance procedures?

## Personnel

1. What are the education, experience, and training of the lab director, supervisors, technicians, and certifying officials?
2. Are sufficient staff employed at each level?

## Records

1. Do chain-of-custody documents exist?
2. Are the details of all initial and confirmatory tests complete and documented?
3. Is a review of each record documented?
4. What is the availability of personnel for attending legal proceedings?

As discussed earlier in this book, the issue of drug testing is under constant review and scrutiny by a wide variety of special-interest groups. There are some noticeable trends that should make most employers happy, but the final verdict has yet to be pronounced. Until that happens, it behooves employers to be very conservative in the use of drug testing. Some believe that the problem of drug abuse in the work force will not disappear until employers are allowed, without restriction, to do random testing. It is our opinion that there is no single solution to this problem. Employers looking for an easy way to deal with substance abuse will not find it in this book. Until something better comes along, we suggest the multidisciplinary approach, which has worked for hundreds of our clients.

# APPENDIX A

## A Synopsis and Explanation of the Employee Polygraph Protection Act of 1988*

### A. GENERAL

On June 27, 1988, President Reagan signed legislation which bars most private employers from using polygraph tests for pre-employment screening, and places such substantial restrictions on the use of polygraphs for current employees that most private sector employers do not find it realistic to continue their use. The person taking the test must be furnished prior notice of numerous specifics regarding the nature of the test, must sign a written statement informing him of numerous specific rights and remedies under the law, must be provided an opportunity to review the specific questions to be asked, and must be allowed to terminate the test at any time. Questions on religious, political, racial, and sexual matters, and union beliefs, are prohibited from being asked. Polygraphs generally should not be administered even if an employee volunteers to take the examination to exonerate himself, since the law not only prohibits employers from indirectly suggesting a polygraph, but also makes it unlawful for any employer "to use, accept, refer to, or inquire concerning the results of" any lie detector test. The law went into effect December 27, 1988.

### B. EXEMPTIONS

The Act allows limited pre-employment testing to continue for those applying for certain security guard positions with employers whose "primary business purpose" is security (see F below). Also permitted, with restrictions, is pre-employment testing by employers who "manufacture, distribute or dispense" controlled substances, with respect to prospective employees who would have direct access to the manufacture, storage, distribution, or sale of those controlled substances (see E below). Public employers are also exempt.

*From "Behind the Front Page," Labor Relations Seminar, 1989; by permission of Alley and Alley, Attorneys at Law, Tampa, Florida.

## C.  THE "ONGOING INVESTIGATION" EXEMPTION

### 1.  Generally

The Act permits testing of current employees as a part of an "ongoing investigation," regardless of the business in which the employer is engaged. Employees who are reasonably suspected of workplace theft or other incidents causing the employer economic loss may be tested, if they had access to the property involved. Before the test can be administered, however, the worker must be given a signed written statement which specifically describes the incident under investigation, the basis for testing particular employees, and the basis of the employer's reasonable suspicion, in addition to other requirements.

### 2.  Specific Incident or Activity

The regulations issued by the Secretary of Labor require that the "ongoing investigation" must be of a "specific incident or activity" and not merely to determine whether or not any thefts have occurred. An employer is also precluded from using this exemption if the ongoing investigation is continuous. As one example, the interim regulations state that a continuing warehouse inventory problem is not sufficient for administering polygraph tests. Even if the employer establishes that unusually high amounts of inventory are missing during a certain period of time, that fact, in and of itself, is not a sufficient basis for administering polygraph tests to an employee "without evidence of intentional wrongdoing." The regulations state that polygraph use in such circumstances "without identification of a specific incident or activity" and a "reasonable suspicion that the employee is involved" would amount to "little more than a fishing expedition."

### 3.  Economic Loss or Injury

The Act cites losses or injuries resulting from theft, embezzlement, misappropriation, unlawful industrial espionage, or sabotage. The regulations state that the list is not exhaustive, and other examples would include "check-kiting, money laundering, or the misappropriation of confidential or trade secret information." However, the regulations also require that "the economic loss must result from intentional wrongdoing" so that "apparently unintentional losses" such as truck, car, or workplace accidents do not give rise to an occasion for polygraphing those involved. Also, according to the regulations, any economic loss resulting from lawful union or employee activity (such as lost business caused by a strike) and any loss to other employees (as opposed to a loss to the employer's business) do not satisfy this requirement.

## 4. No Polygraphs Regarding Drug or Alcohol Use

While the Act does not prohibit medical tests to determine the presence of controlled substances in the body, the interim regulations state that the "ongoing investigation" exemption does not allow an employer to give an employee a polygraph test to learn whether or not he has used drugs or alcohol. This is true even where such possible substance abuse may have contributed to an economic loss to the employer, such as an accident caused by a drunk employee driving a company vehicle.

## 5. Access to Property

The Act requires that in order to polygraph an employee as part of an ongoing investigation into economic loss, the employee to be polygraphed must have had "access" to the property lost. The regulations provide that, under this exemption, "access" includes not only direct, physical access, but less direct access as well. Examples given in the regulations:

> For example, all employees working in or with authority to enter a warehouse storage area have "access" to the property in the warehouse. All employees with the combination to a safe have "access" to the property in a locked safe. Employees also have "access" who have the ability to divert possession or otherwise affect the disposition of the property that is the subject of investigation. For example, a bookkeeper in a jewelry store with access to inventory records may aid or abet a clerk who steals an expensive watch by removing the watch from the employer's inventory records. In such a situation, it is clear that the bookkeeper effectively has "access" to the property that is the subject of the investigation.

## 6. Reasonable Suspicion

The regulations go on to further define the "reasonable suspicion," which an employer must have in order to polygraph an employee as part of an ongoing investigation. "Reasonable suspicion" refers to an "observable, articulate basis in fact" that an employee was involved in or responsible for an economic loss. While "access" or potential opportunity alone does not constitute a basis for "reasonable suspicion," factors such as information from a co-worker or an employee's demeanor or behavior may be a basis for "reasonable suspicion."

## D. PROHIBITION ON DISCIPLINE

1. The Act prohibits an employee from being discharged, dismissed, disciplined, discriminated against, or denied employment or promotion solely on the basis of the results of the test or for refusing to take the test.

2.   The Act provides that an employee may not be disciplined on the basis of a polygraph test report "without additional supporting evidence." The regulations include, as additional supporting evidence, (1) evidence indicating that the employee had access to the property, (2) evidence leading to the employer's reasonable suspicion, or (3) admissions or statements made by the employee before, during, or following the examination. Since there must be evidence of access and evidence providing a "reasonable suspicion" in order to conduct the test, it appears that in some or even many cases, no further evidence will be required. Even so, in light of the penalties provided should a court find that the examination failed to comply with the statute and regulations, it may be safer to discharge an "at will" employee on the basis of the pre-existing evidence, rather than to conduct the examination. The regulations make clear that neither the polygraph result nor the refusal to take a polygraph may serve as a basis for an adverse employment action unless the employer observes "all" the requirements of the Act.

## E.  EXEMPTION FOR MANUFACTURERS AND DISTRIBUTORS

The Act permits limited use of polygraphs by employers authorized to manufacture, distribute, or dispense certain controlled substances. The interim regulations provide that this exemption does not apply to common or contract carriers and warehouses, whose possession of the controlled substance is in the usual course of their business, and who are not required to register with the Drug Enforcement Agency.

## F.  EXEMPTION FOR EMPLOYERS PROVIDING SECURITY SERVICES

1.   Section 7(e) of the Act provides an exemption for companies whose "primary business purpose" consists of providing armored car, security alarm, and security guard services. A company which employs its own security personnel does not qualify. The regulations state that in the case of diversified firms, the term "primary business purpose" means that at least 50% of the employer's annual dollar volume is derived from exempt services.

2.   The Act does not simply permit polygraphing by any such firm; rather, the function of the employer must include the protection of "facilities, materials or operations having a significant impact on" the health or safety of a state, a political subdivision, or the national security of the United States.

3.   The exemption provided under §7(e) of the Act only permits polygraphing of prospective employees employed to protect facilities, materials, operations, or assets as described in the regulations. However, the regulations state that this includes employees who "indirectly" protect such operations. For example, in the armored car industry, a prospective employee who will be taking customer orders for currency and

commodity transfer could be polygraphed, due to the indirect role the prospective employee will have in protection.

4. On the other hand, there are some types of employees in the security industry who "would not be employed to protect" the functions within the exemption and would not have "access" to the process of providing security services. For example, custodial and maintenance employees typically would not have access, either directly or indirectly, to the operations or clients of the employer. The exemption would not extend to such employees.

## G. EXEMPTION FOR PUBLIC EMPLOYERS

The bill exempts federal, state, and local governments and does not apply to certain testing administered by government agencies for national defense or security reasons.

## H. PROCEDURES TO BE FOLLOWED IN CONDUCTING AN EXAMINATION UNDER THE REGULATIONS

### 1. 48 Hours Notice

The "reasonable notice" which must be provided to the employee must be received by the employee at least 48 hours (excluding weekends and holidays) prior to the time of the examination.

### 2. Written Notice

Under the regulations, the written notice to the examinee must be "in a language understood by the examinee." (The regulations do not address examinees who are illiterate in all languages.) The regulations add a number of other requirements, taken from the Act, which must be specifically included in the written notice to the examinee. A suggested "Notice to Examinee" is included as an appendix to the regulations, and is reproduced at the end of this section. Where the polygraph is conducted pursuant to the exemption for ongoing investigations, the employer must give the employee a statement setting forth with "specificity beyond the mere assertion of general statements" regarding the economic loss, the employee's access, and the employer's basis for reasonable suspicion.

## I. REMEDIES

Federal courts have the power to award legal and equitable relief, including employment, reinstatement, promotion, lost wages and benefits, and attorney's fees; and the

Department of Labor may seek civil fines of up to $10,000 against employers who violate the Act.

## J. NOTICES TO BE POSTED

Notwithstanding that most employers will not be using polygraphs at all, the law does require all employers engaged in (or affecting) commerce to post and maintain yet another notice, posted "in conspicuous places on its premises where notices to employees and applicants to employment are customarily posted," which sets forth the pertinent provisions of the Act. Copies of the notices which must be posted in the workplace are available at local offices of the Department of Labor, Wage and Hour Division.

## NOTICE TO EXAMINEE

Section 8(b) of the Employee Polygraph Protection Act, and U.S. Department of Labor regulations (29 CFR 801.22) require that you be given the following information before taking a polygraph examination:

1. (a) The polygraph examination room does/does not contain a two-way mirror, a camera, or another device through which you may be observed.
   (b) Another device, such as those used in conversation or recording will/will not be used during the examination.
   (c) Both you and the employer have the right, with the other's knowledge, to record electronically the entire examination.
2. (a) You have the right to terminate the examination at any time.
   (b) You have the right, and will be given the opportunity, to review all questions to be asked during the tests.
   (c) You will not be asked questions in a manner which degrades or needlessly intrudes.
   (d) You will not be asked any questions concerning: religious beliefs or opinions; beliefs regarding racial matters, political beliefs, or affiliations; matters relating to sexual behavior beliefs, affiliations, opinions, or lawful activities regarding unions and other labor organizations.
   (e) The examination will not be conducted if there is sufficient written evidence by a physician that you are suffering from a medical or psychological condition or undergoing treatment that might cause abnormal response during the examination.
3. (a) The test is not and cannot be required as a condition of employment.
   (b) The employer may not discharge, dismiss, discipline, deny employment or promotion, or otherwise discriminate against you based on the analysis of a polygraph test; or based on your refusal to take such a test without additional evidence which would support such action.
   (c) (1) In connection with an ongoing investigation, the additional evidence required for an employer to take adverse action against you, including termination, may be (A) evidence that you had access to property that is the subject of the investigation, together with (B) the evidence supporting the employer's reasonable suspicion that you were involved in the incident or activity under investigation.
      (2) Any statement made by you before or during the examination may serve as additional supporting evidence for an adverse employment action, as described in 3(b) above, and any admission of criminal conduct by you may be transmitted to an appropriate government law enforcement agency.
4. (a) Information acquired from a polygraph examination may be disclosed by the examiner or by the employer only:
      (1) To you or any other person specifically designated in writing by you to receive such information;

(2) To the employer that requested the test;

(3) To a court, government agency, arbitrator, or mediator that obtains a court order;

(4) To a U.S. Department of Labor official when specifically designated in writing by you to receive such information.

    (a) Information acquired from a polygraph examination may be disclosed by the employer to an appropriate governmental agency without a court order where, and only insofar as, the information disclosed is an admission of criminal conduct.

5. If any of your rights or protections under the law are violated, you have the right to file a complaint with the Wage and Hour Division of the U.S. Department of Labor, or to take action in court against the employer. Employers who violate this law are liable to the affected employee, who may recover such legal equitable relief as may be appropriate, including employment, reinstatement, and promotion, payment of lost wages and benefits, and reasonable costs, including attorney's fees. The Secretary of Labor may also bring action to restrain violations of the Act, or may assess civil money penalties against the employer.

6. Your rights under the Act *may not be waived,* either voluntarily or involuntarily, by contract or otherwise, except as part of a written settlement to a pending action or complaint under the Act, and agreed to and signed by the parties.

I acknowledge that I have received a copy of the above notice, and that it has been read to me.

_____

Date

_____

Signature

# APPENDIX B

## Interview Matrix

Name _____

Date of birth _____ Date of employment _____

Job _____

Shift _____ Identification # _____

Drug _____

Use/On _____

Drug _____

Sale/On _____

Drug _____

Use/Off _____

Drug _____

Sale/Off _____

Drug _____

Possession/On _____

Marijuana

Possession/On _____

Marijuana

Use/On _____

Marijuana

Sale/On _____

Marijuana

Use/Sale/Off _____

Theft _____

Alcohol _____

Miscellaneous _____

(Place page number from Daily Undercover Report next to each item.)

# APPENDIX  C

## Interviewer's Checklist

Confidential Management Services, Inc.

Date _____     Case _____

Subject _____     Interviewer 1 _____

Client Representative _____     Interviewer 2 _____

Union Representative _____

|  | START | STOP |  | START | STOP |
|---|---|---|---|---|---|
| Interview: | _____ | / _____ | Breaks: | _____ | / _____ |
| Written: | _____ | / _____ |  | _____ | / _____ |
| Oral: | _____ | / _____ |  | _____ | / _____ |
| Labor: | _____ | / _____ |  | _____ | / _____ |

(Military time, please)

| Documentation Procedures | Initials | Signatures Obtained | Initials |
|---|---|---|---|
| Tape fidelity | _____ | The subjects | _____ |
| Tab break and foil | _____ | The clients | _____ |
| Employee information sheet | _____ | The union representative | _____ |
| Interviewer notes | _____ | Interviewer 1 | _____ |
| Written checklist | _____ | Interviewer 2 | _____ |
| Written statement | _____ |  |  |
| Addendum statement | _____ |  |  |
| Interviewer statement | _____ |  |  |
| English translation | _____ |  |  |
| Drug worksheets | _____ |  |  |
| Theft worksheets | _____ | Comments: _____ |  |
| Oral checklist | _____ | _____ |  |
| Consent to search | _____ | _____ |  |
| Physical search | _____ | _____ |  |
| Search recovery | _____ | _____ |  |

# APPENDIX  D

## Management Consulting Report

To:       XYZ Company
From:    Confidential Management Services, Inc.
Date:     March 10, 19XX
Subject:  Phase Five Report

As an integral part of the recently concluded activities conducted by Confidential Management Services, Inc., we also interviewed those employees who were identified during the investigation as having been involved in malfeasant activities. The purpose of these secondary interviews was to determine some of the root causes for the employees' aberrant behavior and to analyze their responses in light of industrial behavior studies in order to make recommendations for the company to consider. If implemented, these recommendations will go a long way toward ensuring that the company can rid itself of the problem of drug and alcohol abuse in the workplace and improve productivity. The evidence is clear that the problem of substance abuse and its negative impact on the honesty and productivity of many employees is of major proportions in this country. Unfortunately, the problem's impact on profits is not made clear until it is found in one's own backyard. Not unlike abusers of drugs and alcohol, many companies have difficulty overcoming their denial of the problem and accepting partial responsibility for its presence, which would enable them to attempt the appropriate corrective action.

The XYZ Company has taken the first important steps in detection, confrontation, and discipline of the culpable employees. *It is therefore very important to maintain the initiative and move in the direction of prevention so that the problem does not return.* There are three main factors connected to the presence of malfeasant activity in the workplace. They are:

1.  The quality of employees hired into the work force.
2.  The environment into which the employees are placed (that is, the perceived attitude of management toward its own rules and regulations).
3.  The quality of management (supervision) over the employees.

Fortunately, all three of these areas are within the control of the company. Unfortunately, industry as a whole contemplates the problem of substance abuse only occasionally, when a related incident makes the news (such as the recent traffic accident involving a Rapid Transit District driver found to be a user of cocaine).

Upon hearing such news, we have a tendency to shake our heads, wonder what is becoming of the world, and say how happy we are that we don't have the problem. However, if we are to come to grips with the problem and be counted as leaders in industry and society, we must forsake past practices and take bold corrective action. Companies have the most to gain (or lose) depending on their willingness (or unwillingness) to realistically address the problem and venture forth with strong, consistent steps aimed at a solution. The five-phase approach toward a solution of the problem consists of:

1.  Problem identification and information gathering.
2.  Undercover investigation.
3.  Confrontation.
4.  Disciplinary action.
5.  Preventative measures.

XYZ Company has taken the first steps in its recent activities at the facility in (city). The question remains, however, whether the XYZ Company is going to assume a position of leadership in this critical area of human resource management and reap the ultimate reward in terms of higher productivity, lower costs, and increased profits in all divisions. It is clear that the company cannot continue doing "business as usual," since *the symptoms of the drug and alcohol cancer will reappear and spread throughout the company if the preventative therapy is not applied.*

It is important to consider whether the XYZ Company is setting the best example for its employees relative to proper (i.e., most productive) conduct. According to the comments of employees and managers alike, alcohol is used during work hours by employees at all levels, including executives who indulge in "three-martini lunches." Employees feel justified in taking their lead from the actions of management. The XYZ Company needs to take a long look at its corporate policies and procedures to ensure that they are helping to accomplish the goals of the company.

To take effective measures requires a candid, critical, often unsettling self-examination. It is also true, however, that nothing of lasting value is gained without concerted effort. You have already received the up-to-the-minute results of the "criminal" interviews and have moved in the direction of corrective discipline. Although it is not our intention to rehash them, we believe there is real value in presenting a synopsis of the "industrial behavior" interviews, which have afforded us some insight into the "whys" of some of the malfeasant activities that have occurred on company time and property. It must be kept in mind that we have interfaced with a relatively small percentage of your total work force; therefore, drawing conclusions about the total organization is inappropriate. There are, nonetheless, several recurring themes that need to be addressed. They are both positive and negative.

## On the Positive Side

Generally, the employees interviewed genuinely like the company. They feel that it is a good employer and that the work and pay are to their liking (although most feel that the raises are too few and too small). They feel that the benefits offered by the company are good but were better in the past. On a personal level, they all seem to like the vast majority of the people who work for the XYZ Company. They also feel that the company tries to be fair but that some of the lower-level managers and supervisors (especially leads) don't always do what is expected of them. There appears to be a solid basis upon which to build a close and productive company spirit that will help the XYZ Company become an even more profitable company with excellent employee relations.

## On the Negative Side

Notwithstanding the generally positive feelings about the company, there were strongly held negative feelings about several issues. These issues, it must be stressed, are within the control of management and can therefore be corrected. Specific recommendations for corrective action are made later in this report. The major areas of concern include:

1. Employment
2. Discipline
3. Communication
4. Wages and Benefits
5. Favoritism

We present here a distillation of the comments made on each of these areas by those interviewed.

## Employment

The subject of employment has been touched on in previous conversations with company representatives, including a recommendation that some training be conducted by Confidential Management Services, Inc.

The XYZ Company is already aware of the need for more selective hiring practices. It is therefore suggested that the company require all those involved in hiring (including Personnel Department staff and line managers who conduct interviews) to participate in refresher training in the best methods for interviewing from both the security and human-resources perspectives. The best time to solve problems with employees is at the front door, before they become part of the work force.

## Discipline

The following comments are specifically relevant to the use of drugs in the workplace but also relate to overall discipline.

> It is too lax and unequal. Don't make it like a prison here, but it should be more firm. My supervisor seems to be too busy to notice the drugs—At least he never said anything about it to make me think he cared.

They are too lax until the "last straw." A lot of people are slacking—"Why work more than they make you" seems to be the thought of a lot of my co-workers. About the drugs: Dorothy knew there was a problem, and she tried to make subtle suggestions to me to clean up my act, but maybe she was trying to be too much of a friend and not tough enough to really help. The leadman, Alex, is a big problem; he just laughs at you and mocks you if you do something wrong. He never leaves you with your dignity.

The company—especially the guards—see what is going on [with the drugs], but they don't do anything. They need to nip it in the bud. This investigation is one of the best things that ever happened to the XYZ Company. I would do the same thing [investigate]. I only hope they keep it up and not let things fall back to normal. They also need to be more consistent in their discipline.

They knew there was a problem with drugs, but they didn't do anything unless a person was caught red-handed. The lax discipline and the fact that some employees think they are too sly to get caught is why they think they can get away with doing drugs.

Discipline concerning production is tight. I mean, they are on top of you about your work level. But they are pretty lax on discipline about behavior. Even if they know or suspect that someone is using drugs, they take no action.

Even my supervisor is involved in this. When he was a leadman, I did him a favor and provided him with marijuana. [The supervisor later told this to his interviewer from Confidential Management Services, Inc.]

They [management] know [about the drugs], but they never do anything about it. They just turn their backs on the problem.

I was never disciplined about my lateness problem; I just straightened it out myself. The guards and the supervisors never walk around to see what is going on. They [the bosses] should get out and around more and talk to us. They need to be more on top of things.

I am not sure, but I think the supervisors know about the drugs. But they never say anything.

## Communication

One minute it's do this, next minute it's do that, then the next minute it's do this again. It gets very frustrating. You feel like you are treated like a machine, without any respect for you as a person. They really need to improve on communication.

With Figueroa you had to be very argumentative just to get anything done. He made you feel like you were always wrong. The new one [supervisor] is much better, so far. They never really come right out and talk to you; they just kind of drop hints and are too subtle.

It could be much better if management would be a little more up front with us—such as with Tucson—to stop rumors with straight facts. People are very tense about the future and their jobs with the company. Please get the company to stop "shinning us on" and really talk to us. Get involved and let the employees know you are working *with* them. Give more advance notice of layoffs or changes.

The morale is a little low now because there is confusion over the move to Tucson.

My supervisor is too busy to talk to me.

We have meetings, but no communication. There is no give and take or exchange of ideas. We work on rumors only. For example, Is the company going to move to Arizona? Are we going to be out of a job? We're in a period of very low morale now. Everyone is out for themselves in a dog-eat-dog way.

No one knows what's really going on. There are no thank-you's for a good job, no recognition for extra effort—it makes you feel like a piece of shit. You really feel like they are shinning you on when you do them a favor and are told you will get recognition for it in a raise, or at least a pat on the back, and then you hear nothing.

Communication is poor. They really don't talk with us. I am really worried about the future with the company and their plans about the move. Let us know what is happening; get us more involved in the company.

Rumors fly around. The meetings help, but they don't really encourage true open communication.

## Wages and Benefits

They changed the way we were given raises recently and made it very unfair. For example, the lower-paid people got a 3 percent raise and the higher-paid people got a 5 percent raise. Now, I ask you: Is it fair to raise the people who make the most money in the first place by a higher percent than you raise the lower people, who could really use the extra money?

The way they messed up the wages and two-tiered the increases got a lot of people upset.

Wages and benefits are pretty reasonable, but they used to be a lot better, and it seems to be an indication of how they feel about us now.

You get no merit for doing a better job. No matter what you do, the guy next to you is going to get the same amount. There is no incentive to be better than the next guy or to do extra.

## Favoritism

It used to be a lot worse under Figueroa, when there was extreme favoritism.

Some supervisors use favoritism, and they [the company] bring people from the outside for some of the better jobs instead of letting people here bid on it.

Figueroa's second cousin Alex was brought in, and I trained him in everything he knows, and he was made leadman. He is totally incompetent and does not have the company's interests at heart.

He [Alex] stood by and laughed when a machine was burning and did nothing to put out the fire.

Some people are given second chances and others are not, even though they do the same things.

## Analysis and Recommendations

Taken by themselves, these statements could be discouraging; however, they point out again that appropriate action can bring about remedies that will help reduce employee-related problems and improve productivity and therefore profits. The question becomes, What should be done?

It is evident, on the surface, that the aforementioned areas are closely related to one another and, although addressed individually, are all part of the overall issue of management development. It might be helpful for the company to undertake a management audit to determine whether the first- and second-line managers and supervisors are the best-qualified people for the positions they hold. Such an audit might also indicate who could be doing a better job with some additional training. The audit could take the form of interviews conducted by Confidential Management Services, Inc., under the pretense of following up on the investigation with the leads and foremen.

The area of discipline is a critical one. As indicated by the comments of the culpable employees, even they would appreciate stronger discipline. The policies are in place but are obviously not being followed. Supervisors and managers need to be fully versed in the company's policies and procedures and trained in the proper techniques for correcting improper behavior. There is a need for ongoing reinforcement in this area of management development. Regular seminars are called for on how to recognize improper actions and the methods for correcting them, including corrective interviewing and the exercise of judgment.

Communication is more than just giving orders or talking to people. It involves a two-way effort and a desire to establish a positive relationship with others. This is not meant to imply that it is the job of management to make employees feel better or that there is anything to be gained by making the XYZ Company a "country club." Quite the contrary; the result of effective communication is that everyone knows what is expected of him or her. The key is to make certain that supervisors treat people with respect—that they recognize that regardless of the job a person holds, he or she has worth and is to be valued. It is amazing how effective this simple thought can be when applied. Everyone wants to be thought of as being worth the attention of his or her boss.

It is unfortunate that people in management at all levels are often shackled by the belief that they can't talk to their subordinates. They are often afraid that they will be rejected or will say or do something wrong if they talk to their employees, so they ignore them. The result is that both employees and supervisors feed a self-fulfilling prophecy, and after a while they *can't* talk to each other.

The area of management training has been touched on in the foregoing comments. The need is for an effective program that has thorough follow-through from upper levels of management to ensure that the training applies to the company's day-to-day operations in practical ways. One way is to have all levels of management partake in similar training so that they have a common ground to work from and can reinforce the positive aspects of the training. Also, upper management needs to incorporate in its performance evaluations of the supervisors (and managers at all levels) a critical review of the management style and the degree to which problems are solved before they become serious. This requires a close relationship between the people at all levels of the organization (in effect, good management techniques from everyone). Since most managers have risen from the ranks (either here or elsewhere), many have never been given training in the management techniques so essential to the successful completion of their assigned responsibilities. This is true no matter how much other education they have received. Since companies stand to benefit from the skills of their managers, it is in the interest of companies to provide management training.

Middle and lower-level managers are a vital link in any organization because they have a direct impact on profits and problem solving. Unfortunately, as a group (nationally, not just in the XYZ Company), they are the people worst prepared to meet the demands placed on them in today's society.

The management philosophy and follow-through of the company from the top down can set a tone of commitment to excellence that spreads throughout the organization and helps to ensure that a repeat of the just-completed investigation will not have to happen soon. Study after study has proven that the improvement of employee performance in a company is best accomplished when it is consistently pursued over a long period of time. There is no overnight cure-all; a patient and persistent effort pays the highest return.

As we have stated, control over the XYZ Company's problems is in the hands of its management. This requires management to make a critical self-evaluation and accept the responsibility for making the company better. By taking initiative and forging ahead, management demonstrates that it is in charge and that "the inmates are not running the asylum."

A strong message should be sent throughout the organization: this is a great place to work because we have our act together. The key is follow-through on a day-to-day basis. As seen by the comments of some of the "worst" employees, even they would welcome it. And they are not fooled by rhetoric; they want to see action. The single most important influence on productivity and, therefore, profits is the human factor, and the degree to which it is improved rests with management. The ball is in your court.

Specifically, we recommend that the XYZ Company undertake a program that will build a sense of unity in the organization from the top down. In order to get the most mileage from such an effort, it should be coordinated and have a relationship to the needs of the employees as they perceive them. Therefore, an in-depth employee opinion survey that gives the employees a chance to air their feelings in a positive way and allows management to gain valuable input would be a good first step. It would show the employees that management really cares about their feelings and wants help in making the company a better place for all. Management would be able to develop programs on the basis of information revealed by the survey. It might be pointed out here that the XYZ Company has many of the signs typically seen in a company with a high level of employee unrest, which often leads to a union-organizing attempt.

The survey will suggest the direction that the company should pursue and ensure that the funds spent on management development are spent in the proper areas. The insights gained as a result of the Phase Five interviews are valuable; however, it should be kept in mind that they are the results of talking to only the small percentage of the total work force that was caught up in the problem being investigated. On the other hand, the survey will allow for all employees to share their comments with management and will show how widespread the discontent is. Several of the employees we interviewed commented that they wanted the company to do well but were frustrated, and being able to share their opinions and ideas anonymously was a good outlet for them.

Specific training in the areas of employment, discipline, and management development should be considered by the XYZ Company as a valuable means of preventing the recurrence of the problems uncovered while at the same time increasing productivity. A brief outline of suggested training follows.

We have enjoyed working with you to this point and look forward to helping you in your efforts toward improving on past successes while pointing toward the future.

## EMPLOYMENT TRAINING

1. Introduction of facilitator and participants.
2. Discovery on the part of the participants of the need for employment policies and procedures.
3. Development of employment policies and procedures (along the lines of present policies).
4. Experience with writing meaningful "Request for Employee" memoranda to ensure effective assistance from the Personnel Department.
5. Review of the employment application form and items to look for when screening applicants. Practice in ranking candidates.
6. Brainstorming do's and don'ts of interviewing. Practice in writing open-ended, unbiased questions (discussion of Equal Employment Opportunity Commission and Fair Employment and Housing Commission guidelines).
7. Role-playing in practice interviews based on the XYZ Company situations.
8. Critique of training; evaluation of objectives.

## DISCIPLINARY TRAINING

1. Introduction of facilitator and participants.
2. Needs analysis and statement of objectives for the training (developed by the participants).
3. Discovery on the part of the participants of the reasons for a disciplinary policy.
4. Delegation of the responsibility for discipline.
5. Development and communication of rules and standards of behavior.
6. Types of misconduct:
   a. Serious misconduct (calling for immediate discipline).
   b. Other misconduct (including not working up to accepted standards).
7. Enforcement steps:
   a. Verbal warning.
   b. Written warning.
   c. Suspension and discharge.

8.  The disciplinary interview.
9.  Follow-through to corrected behavior or dismissal.


## MANAGEMENT TRAINING

 1.  Evolution of management with changes in society.
 2.  Motivation: what it is and isn't.
 3.  Recognition and development of perceptions and attitudes.
 4.  Managing morale and group dynamics.
 5.  Effective management: when to lead, when to "boss."
 6.  Participative management and productivity: when, why, how.
 7.  Managing change: understanding resistance.
 8.  Management by objective: advantages and drawbacks.
 9.  Goal setting and feedback: effective communication.
10.  Developing organizational teamwork.

# APPENDIX E

## Statement Forms

Confidential Management Services, Inc.

Page 1 of \_\_\_\_\_

Statement of _____

Business address _____ Phone ( \_\_\_\_\_ ) _____

Home address _____ Phone ( \_\_\_\_\_ ) _____

1. I, _____ , hereby make the following
2. declaration to _____ , who has identified
3. himself/herself to me as a private investigator from Confidential Management
4. Services, Inc. No threats or promises have been made to me to induce me to make
5. this declaration, which I hereby acknowledge is made of my own free will.
6. _____
7. _____
8. _____
9. _____
10. _____
11. _____
12. _____
13. _____
14. _____
15. _____
16. _____

Date _____

Employee _____        _____
          (signature)                           (print name)

Witness _____        _____
          (signature)                           (print name)

Witness _____        _____
          (signature)                           (print name)

Confidential Management Services, Inc.

Page _____ of _____

Statement of _____

1. _____
2. _____
3. _____
4. _____
5. _____
6. _____
7. _____
8. _____
9. _____
10. _____
11. _____
12. _____
13. _____
14. _____
15. _____
16. _____

Date _____

Employee _____       _____
          (signature)                  (print name)
Witness _____       _____
          (signature)                  (print name)
Witness _____       _____
          (signature)                  (print name)

Confidential Management Services, Inc.

Page _____ of _____

Statement of _____

1. _____
2. _____
3. _____
4. _____
5. _____
6. _____
7. _____
8. _____
9. _____
10. _____
11. _____
12. _____
13. _____
14. _____
15. _____
16. _____

I have read the above _____ lines and declare under and knowing the penalty for perjury that they are true and correct. I (have) (have not) (circle one) requested representation to date.

Signed at _____ , _____ , _____ ,
            (company)                      (city)                 (county)

CA, this _____ day of _____ , 19XX.

Employee _____          _____
              (signature)                         (print name)

Witness _____          _____
              (signature)                         (print name)

Witness _____          _____
              (signature)                         (print name)

# APPENDIX F

## Written Declaration Checklist

Confidential Management Services, Inc.

Interviewer _____    Interview Start _____

Subject _____    Interview Finish _____

Client Witness _____    Written Start _____

Date _____    Written Finish _____

_____ Checked with coordinator and other interviewers for more information.

_____ Opening paragraph.

_____ Established subject's malfeasance.
(Since I began working for the company, I . . . )

_____ Established first and last times malfeasance committed, and where.

_____ Established malfeasance of others.
(I know the following people have . . . )

_____ Established motive for subject's actions.
(The reason I was involved in these problems was that . . . )

_____ Established that subject realizes he/she violated company policy and/or criminal law or code.
(I know that I have violated company policy and the law . . . )

_____ Established that subject realizes that because of above, he/she could possibly be terminated and/or prosecuted.
(I also know that because of this I could be terminated and/or prosecuted.)

_____ Established what motive subject had for being truthful, despite knowing the above.
(Nevertheless, I was truthful because . . . )

_____ Established how subject would like company to handle the problem. (I would like the company to . . . )

_____ Obtained subject's commitment to not repeat malfeasance, regardless of the outcome. (Regardless of the outcome, whether I continue to work here or elsewhere, I promise I will never again . . . )

_____ Provided subject opportunity to add anything in his/her own words, or established that he/she had nothing to add in his/her own words. (I have been given the opportunity to add anything to this statement in my own words, and . . . )

_____ Took closing statement as declaration.

_____ Had all parties present sign statement.

NOTE: Before moving on to the oral declaration, determine whether a consent search is appropriate. If it is, obtain one and have subject complete it.

# APPENDIX   G

## Oral Declaration Checklist

Confidential Management Services, Inc.

Interviewer _____     Oral Start _____

Subject _____     Finish _____

Client Witness _____     Date _____

_____   Established that subject understands English.

_____   Identified self and others present, time, date, place; satisfied Penal Code
          section dealing with invasion of privacy.

_____   Established who, what, where, how, and why (re: the investigation).

_____   Explained that investigation started "some time ago" (without specifics).

_____   Confirmed that subject was never told exactly when investigation started.

_____   Determined whether subject has sustained any physical injury recently (on or
          off the job).

_____   Determined whether subject has any mental or emotional problems that
          would preclude his or her being interviewed.

_____   Established that subject understands perjury.

_____   Established two reasons for taping.

_____   Established subject's knowledge of recording.

_____   Established that subject was treated fairly, *and why* (narrative response).

_____   Established we are private investigators and not police.

_____   Established that subject understands employer's right and reason to investi-
          gate, *and why.*

_____   Established that subject was not imprisoned, *and why.*

145

_____ Established that subject did (not) request counsel.

_____ Established that subject was not denied telephone access.

_____ Established that subject was not denied food access.

_____ Established that subject was not denied restroom access.

_____ Established why subject did (not) want representation.

_____ Established the five methods that could be used during an investigation.

_____ Established that investigative information was gathered using "one or more" of the five methods.

_____ Established what subject had been told about legal electronic investigation.

_____ Established two conditions of interview ("regardless").

_____ Established that interviewers are only information gatherers.

_____ Established that employer is the only decision maker.

_____ Established why coercion is not possible.

_____ Established the possibility of termination and/or prosecution. ("Regardless of whether I continue to work here or not.")

_____ Established why subject was truthful, knowing the possibility of termination and/or prosecution.

_____ Brought in any other interviewers to clarify their portion.

_____ Had subject read written statement into tape recorder.

_____ Read Employee Information Sheet into tape recorder.

_____ Clarified the issue of "used with"; be specific. Identified actual users, one or both parties (if necessary).

_____ Allowed client to ask question(s).

_____ Asked client to await final results of investigation before making any decisions concerning disciplinary action.

_____ Gave the subject opportunity to add anything to oral declaration.

_____ Expressed gratitude for cooperation, noting that the act itself cannot be condoned (only if subject was cooperative).

_____ If interview proceeded beyond a reasonable length of time, stated why.

_____ Admonished subject not to discuss the interview or investigation with others, pending completion of case.

_____ Advised the subject that the employer's *intent* is to keep all information confidential between the subject and client. It is possible that this information may be released, if deemed necessary, by the client for use in various matters, such as unemployment hearings, grievances, arbitration, and civil or criminal proceedings.

_____ Client should advise subject of his/her status pending completion of case (meet with management consultant, if applicable).

_____ Covered consent to search, if appropriate.

_____ Took oral statement as a declaration.

_____ "I (*subject states full name*) declare, under and knowing the penalty for perjury, that the oral statement that has just been provided by me is true and correct."

_____ Acknowledged that tape recorder was not turned off during interview.

_____ Established time, date, and place (county and state) tape was turned off.

_____ Before excusing employee, checked with coordinator and supervisor.

NOTE: The objective of the oral interview is to record the subject's *narrative responses* to all the above issues.

# APPENDIX  H

## Operative's Report Checklist

Confidential Management Services, Inc.

(Report when, who, where, what, how, and why about the following:)

INSTRUCTIONS: Use the subtitles in this checklist as the titles for each paragraph in your daily written report to your case supervisor. Number each paragraph in your report with the corresponding number from this checklist. Use "Notes to File" for material and information that does not fit within this format. Reports are made daily, with NO exceptions.

I.  DISHONESTY
1.  Collusive theft
2.  Espionage
3.  Fraudulent exchanges
4.  Fraudulent refunds
5.  Kickbacks
6.  Method of theft
7.  Padded expenditures
8.  Possible theft
9.  Price alterations
10. Questionable activities/ behavior
11. Talk of theft
12. Theft of merchandise/ cash
13. Unauthorized discounts
14. Unauthorized substitutions (merchandise or products)
15. Shortage from vendors
16. Shortage to customers
17. Insurance fraud
18. Talk of police, undercover, or security police activities

II.  PHYSICAL SECURITY
1.  Alarms and time locks
2.  Cash office security
3.  Cash register security
4.  Closed-circuit TV
5.  Computer access and security
6.  Employee identification
7.  Employee respect for security
8.  Exit security
9.  Fences and enclosures
10. File access
11. Fire exits and fire stations
12. Fire prevention
13. Guard systems
14. Information security
15. Key control
16. Lock-up practices
17. Night security
18. Pass system for merchandise removal
19. Persons in unauthorized areas
    a.  Customers and others
    b.  Employees
20. Roof and skylight security

21. Sabotage of equipment/
    merchandise
22. Sealing or locking of trucks
23. Shipping and receiving dock
    security
24. Storage of materials (safe/
    unsafe)
25. Telephone security
26. Tool room/tool control
27. Vehicular security
28. Accidents/injuries

III. EMPLOYEE MALFEASANCE
1. Absenteeism
2. Arguing or fighting
3. Careless handling of property
4. Drinking (alcohol)
5. Eating in work area
6. False production records
7. False time records
8. Failure to cooperate
9. Failure to follow procedures
10. Failure to follow instructions
11. Favoritism (by employees)
12. Fraternization
13. Gambling
14. Hard drugs (sale/use)
15. Idling (or lack of work)
16. Insubordination
17. Lack of cleanliness/
    appearance
18. Leaving early
19. Loansharking
20. Marijuana (sale/use)
21. Markdowns
22. Misuse of company material
23. Misuse of company vehicles
24. Misappropriation of company
    equipment and materials
25. Poor customer service
26. Possession of a weapon
27. Profanity/obscenity
28. Rowdiness
29. Smoking in unauthorized areas
30. Talk of hard drug sale/use
31. Talk of marijuana sale/use

32. Tardiness
33. Unauthorized/overstayed
    breaks
34. Unauthorized phone calls
35. Sabotage
36. Sexual harassment
37. Working under influence of
    drugs or alcohol
38. Driving under influence of
    drugs or alcohol
39. Possible drug activity
40. Sleeping on company time

IV. SUPERVISION
1. Employee respect for
   management
2. Favoritism
3. Indoctrination
4. Lack of supervision
5. Overstaffing
6. Poor housekeeping
7. Poor scheduling
8. Poor or nonexistent records
9. Poor customer service
10. Poor supervisory judgment
11. Poor production records
12. Training/orientation
13. Unnecessary overtime
14. Nepotism
15. Job description of operative
16. Discrimination
17. Respect for supervisory
    judgment

V. EMPLOYER-EMPLOYEE
   RELATIONS
1. Attitude toward management
2. Awareness of employee rights
3. Bonuses
4. Discrimination
5. Effects of policy changes
6. Employees' job attitudes
7. Facilities and benefits
   a. Discounts
   b. Washrooms
   c. Cafeteria

d. Parties
e. Medical
f. Insurance
g. Pension
h. Incentives
8. Function of Personnel
Department
    a. Hiring
    b. Firing
    c. Screening
    d. Training
    e. Handling employee
        complaints
9. Labor turnover
10. Messages from management
11. Compliance with
    Occupational Safety and
    Health Act regulations
12. Overtime
13. Promotions
14. Rumors
15. Suggestion system
16. Customer opinion of client/
    employee
17. Supplier opinion of client/
    employee
18. Customer complaints
19. Probation

VI. EVALUATION OF
    EMPLOYEES
    1. Abilities
    2. Ambitions
    3. Attendance record
    4. Character
    5. Conscientiousness

6. Courtesy
7. Drinking
8. Education
9. Family
10. Friendliness
11. Friends
12. Hobbies
13. Honesty
14. Illnesses
15. Integrity
16. Leadership
17. Morals
18. Past criminal record
19. Past employment
20. Personal appearance
21. Personality traits
22. Physical characteristics
23. Possessions
24. Potential
25. Special interests
26. Talents
27. Value to company
28. Work habits
29. Willingness to train others
30. General attitude of the work
    force
31. Attitude toward co-workers
32. Residence
33. Vehicle

VII. NEW SYSTEMS AND
     PROCEDURES
     (Report accordingly)

VIII. LUNCH
      (Report with one of the
      aforementioned sections)

# APPENDIX I

## Drug and Alcohol Policy

### I. PURPOSES

The purposes of this policy are as follows:

1. To establish and maintain a safe, healthful working environment for all employees;
2. To reduce the incidence of accidental injury to person or property;
3. To reduce absenteeism, tardiness, and indifferent job performance;
4. To provide assistance toward rehabilitation for any employee who seeks the company's help in overcoming addiction to, dependence on, or problems with alcohol or drugs.

### II. ILLEGAL DRUGS, LEGAL DRUGS, AND ALCOHOL

*Illegal Drugs.* The use, possession, sale, offer to sell, transfer, or purchase of illegal drugs while on company business or on company premises or property is prohibited. Violation of this rule will result in disciplinary action, up to and including termination. Termination is likely for a violation of this rule, even for a first offense.

*Illegal drug* means any drug (a) that is not legally obtainable or (b) that is legally obtainable but has not been legally obtained. The term includes marijuana. It includes prescription drugs not legally obtained and prescription drugs not being used for prescribed purposes. It also includes any substance that a person holds out to another as an illegal drug.

No employee shall bring drug paraphernalia onto company premises or property or into company vehicles. Drug paraphernalia includes pipes, bongs, rolling papers, and other items used in the ingestion or consumption of illegal drugs.

*Legal Drugs.* Legal drugs include prescription drugs and over-the-counter drugs that have been legally obtained and are being used for the purpose for which they were prescribed and manufactured.

No prescription drug shall be brought onto company premises by any person other than the person for whom the drug is prescribed by a licensed medical practitioner. Such drugs shall be used only in the manner, combination, and quantity prescribed.

The use, possession, sale, offer to sell, transfer, or purchase of legal drugs, except under the conditions specifically permitted herein, is prohibited. Violation of this policy can result in disciplinary action, up to and including termination, even for a first offense.

If an employee has any question or concern as to his or her ability to safely or efficiently perform his or her job while taking a prescription drug or other medication, the employee has an obligation to report the use of that drug or medication to _____, who will contact the company physician for a determination of the ability of the employee to work while using that drug. In this case, an employee may continue to work, even while taking a legal drug, if the company has determined, after consulting with its physician, that the employee does not pose a threat to his or her own safety or the safety of co-workers and that the employee's job performance is not significantly affected by the legal drug. Otherwise, the employee may be required to take a leave of absence or comply with other appropriate action determined by management.

Failure to report legal drugs to your supervisor so that a determination of fitness to work can be made can result in disciplinary action, up to and including termination.

*Alcohol.*   No alcoholic beverages may be brought onto or consumed on company premises, except that moderate consumption of alcohol at designated company gatherings or under circumstances expressly authorized by the company will be permitted.

Otherwise, the use of alcoholic beverages on company premises or property or while on company business is prohibited. Violation of this rule can result in disciplinary action, up to and including termination, even for a first offense.

## III.   PROHIBITION AGAINST EMPLOYEES' HAVING ILLEGAL DRUGS OR ALCOHOL IN THEIR BODIES DURING WORKING TIME

All employees of the company are expected to report for work with no illegal drugs or their metabolites or alcohol in their bodies. Employees must not have illegal drugs or their metabolites or alcohol in their bodies at any time while on the job, except when moderate consumption of alcohol is authorized by the company under the circumstances provided in section II of this policy. Compliance with these rules is considered an essential job qualification for all employees.

## IV.   ENFORCEMENT OF RULE PROHIBITING EMPLOYEES FROM HAVING ILLEGAL DRUGS OR ALCOHOL IN THEIR BODIES DURING WORKING TIME

*Pre-employment Alcohol/Drug Screening.*   Prior to employment with the company, all final candidates will be required to pass an alcohol/drug screening test administered by a medical facility designated by the company. Any prospective employee refusing to submit to such examination will not be hired by the company. Any prospective employee failing the alcohol/drug screening test will no longer be considered for employment with the company.

*Reasonable Suspicion Alcohol/Drug Screening.* When the company has a reasonable suspicion that an employee is, or may be, impaired or affected on the job by alcohol or illegal drugs, and when the company has a reasonable suspicion that alcohol or illegal drugs are, or may be, present in an employee's body in violation of the rules set forth above, the employee will be required to submit to an alcohol/drug screening test immediately upon demand by the company. Refusal to submit to such a test amounts to insubordination and shall be sufficient grounds for dismissal. Any employee failing such a test will be subject to dismissal from employment with the company.

A reasonable suspicion may arise from the circumstances of a particular accident or injury occurring on the job; from a physical altercation between employees; from obvious impairment of physical or mental abilities, such as slurred speech or difficulty in maintaining balance; from unexplained significant deterioration in job performance or behavior, such as excessive absenteeism; from reports by co-workers of on-the-job alcohol or drug use or impairment; from employee admissions regarding alcohol or drug use; or from any other evidence reasonably giving rise to suspicion of on-the-job impairment from or use of alcohol or illegal drugs.

## V. EMPLOYEE ASSISTANCE PROGRAM

Any employee who feels that he or she has developed an addiction to, dependence on, or problem with alcohol or drugs, legal or illegal, is encouraged to seek assistance. Assistance may be sought by writing in confidence to, or asking for a personal appointment with, _____, Human Resources Manager.

Each request for assistance will be treated as confidential. Only those persons with a "need to know" will be made aware of such requests.

Human Resources will develop contacts with local hospitals and community organizations offering alcohol or drug treatment programs. Human Resources will refer employees seeking assistance to an appropriate treatment organization.

Rehabilitation itself is the responsibility of the employee. However, any employee seeking medical attention for alcoholism or drug addiction will be entitled to benefits available under the company's group medical insurance plans, with the restrictions and limits stated in the applicable plan summary. Employees on rehabilitation leave will be subject to the extended sick leave and personal leave-of-absence provisions in the Employee Handbook.

To be eligible for continuation in employment following rehabilitation, the employee must provide certification that he or she was continuously enrolled in a treatment program and actively participated in that program. Any employee suffering from an alcohol or drug problem who rejects treatment or who leaves a treatment program prior to being properly discharged therefrom will be dismissed from employment. No employee will be eligible for this employee assistance program more than one time. The recurrence of an alcohol or drug problem will be cause for dismissal.

All employees returning to active employment from rehabilitation will be required to sign a "Return to Work Agreement" providing:

1. For unannounced testing for a period of six months to ensure that the employee is free from the alcohol or drug problem;
2. That failure of such a test during this period shall be grounds for immediate dismissal;
3. That the employee must maintain an acceptable attendance and peformance record and comply with all other company policies upon his or her return to work.

No disciplinary action will be issued against any employee who brings his or her problem to the attention of the company prior to the company's learning of a violation of the drug and alcohol policy. However, if the company has previously verified a violation of the drug and alcohol policy, the company is not obligated to grant the employee rehabilitation leave. Disciplinary action up to and including dismissal may be imposed regardless of whether the employee is offered or accepts rehabilitation leave.

## VI.   SEARCHES

In order to ensure the safety of the workplace and the work force and to protect and preserve company property, the company may from time to time inspect company vehicles, toolboxes, lockers, desks, and file cabinets. These searches may be unannounced, and employees should have no expectation of privacy with respect to items brought onto company property or stored in such company facilities. It is a condition of employment for employees to cooperate with these searches. Refusal to consent to such a search amounts to insubordination and may constitute cause for termination.

In addition, when the company has a reasonable suspicion that an employee or group of employees may be in the possession of drugs or alcohol on company premises or while on company business, they may be required as a condition of employment to submit to reasonable searches of their clothing, their purses, lunchboxes, briefcases, or other containers, or their personal vehicles that are on company property.

## VII.   EFFECTIVE DATE

This policy is effective immediately upon notice to employees. Each present employee will be furnished with a copy of this policy and will sign a receipt for same. Employees hired later will each be furnished with a copy at or before the time of hiring.

## ACKNOWLEDGMENT OF RECEIPT
## OF COMPANY DRUG AND ALCOHOL POLICY

I hereby acknowledge receipt of a copy of the (company name) Drug and Alcohol Policy. I understand that I am responsible for reading the policy and that I must comply with the policy in all respects.

Date _____          _____

(employee signature)

# APPENDIX  J

## Telephone Application Form

Confidential Management Services, Inc.

Name _____     Date _____
Address _____     Telephone _____
City/State/Zip _____

Currently working? (Y/N) _____ If so, where? _____
Work experience _____
_____
_____
_____

Investigative experience _____
_____
_____

Willing to travel?    Local _____     Out of area _____
Languages _____
Special skills/licenses _____
Machinery/equipment _____
Vehicle (make/model/year) _____
Insurance _____
Education:    Graduated High School (Y/N) _____     Year _____
Other schools attended _____
_____

Rating (1–5): _____     Communication skills: _____
Client workplace demographics (B/W/A/H/O) _____

# APPENDIX K

## Client Checklist

Confidential Management Services, Inc.

Client name _____     Date _____
Client address _____     Phone _____

I.  Company Background

    Product/service _____

    When started _____

    President's name _____

    Profitability _____

    Number of employees _____

    Ethnic distribution _____

    Number of shifts and hours _____

    Non-union/union (which) _____

    Employee relations _____

    Last time new employee hired _____

    Last person terminated (why) _____

    Ever used undercover before _____

    Long-term plans _____

II.  Job Description

    Type position _____

    Job description _____

    Supervision _____

    Shift/hours _____

    Pay rate _____

How paid/when _____

Overtime _____

Special policy _____

III.  Qualifications of Operative

Undercover experience _____

Languages _____

IV.  Hiring Procedures

Type hire (cold/controlled) _____

Interview/physical _____

Previous employment verified _____

Job application _____

Start date _____

V.  Policies and Procedures

Procedure manual _____

Posted policies _____

Security checks and badges _____

VI.  Liability and Exposure

Labor attorney _____

Worker compensation _____

Unemployment _____

Medical/dental _____

Liability _____

Fidelity _____

VII.  Miscellaneous

Cast of characters (suspects) _____

_____

_____

Contacting operative _____

Did client contact three previous clients of

agency?   Yes _____   No_____

Compliance with Health and Safety Code re: police agency _____

# APPENDIX L

## Consent to Search

Confidential Management Services, Inc.

I, _____ , Social Security # _____ ,
hereby consent to allow _____ of _____
_____ to search my (person/resident/vehicle/office/other) _____ ,
_____ which is located at_____ .
The purpose of this search is to (remove/recover) _____
_____ .

I certify that the above consent has been freely given by me and that no promises or
threats have been made to me to induce me to sign this consent.

I further agree that the above-named individual(s) may enter the above-described loca-
tion(s) and that I will make no claim whatsoever against the above-named person(s),
Confidential Management Services, Inc., or its officers and employees, in connection
with the entry, search, and/or seizure from the above-described locations.

Date/Time _____        Signature _____

Witness _____
                        (signature and title)
Witness _____
                        (signature and title)

## Confidential Management Services, Inc.

## SEARCH, RECOVERY INVENTORY

In conjunction with the consent to search signed this date, I, _____

_____ , Social Security # _____

hereby release to _____ of Confidential

Management Services, Inc., and _____

of _____ , the following items

recovered as a result of the above mentioned search:

_____

_____

_____

_____

_____

_____

_____

_____

_____

I certify that the above items were surrendered freely by me. Further I will make no claim whatsoever against the person(s) named in the consent to search in connection with the entry, search, and/or seizure from the premises described in the consent to search.

Date/Time _____ Signature _____

Witness _____
                          (signature and title)

Witness _____
                          (signature and title)

# APPENDIX M

## Waiver

### Confidential Management Services, Inc.

I, _____, have been advised of my right to have a union representative present with me during this inquiry. I have or have not (circle one) requested representation at this time.

I have now agreed to continue this interview for an unspecified period of time. In no way has the interviewer talked me out of having a union person here, and I know I can have union representation present as soon as I make the request.

I also reserve the right to discontinue this interview at any time and not continue with the interview until such time as union representation is present.

Signature _____

Date _____

Time _____

Witness _____
        (signature and title)

# APPENDIX N

## Drug-Free Workplace Act of 1988

### Section 5152. Drug-free Workplace Requirements for Federal Contractors

(a) Drug-Free Workplace Requirement.

   (1) *Requirement for Persons Other Than Individuals.* No person, other than an individual, shall be considered a responsible source, under the meaning of such term as defined in section 4(8) of the Office of Federal Procurement Policy Act (41 USC 403(8)), for the purposes of being awarded a contract for the procurement of any property or services of a value of $25,000 or more from any Federal agency unless such person has certified to the contracting agency that it will provide a drug-free workplace by

     (A) publishing a statement notifying employees that the unlawful manufacture, distribution, dispensation, possession, or use of a controlled substance is prohibited in the person's workplace and specifying the actions that will be taken against employees for violations of such prohibition;

     (B) establishing a drug-free awareness program to inform employees about

       (i) the dangers of drug abuse in the workplace;

       (ii) the person's policy of maintaining a drug-free workplace;

       (iii) any available drug counseling, rehabilitation, and employee assistance programs; and

       (iv) the penalties that may be imposed upon employees for drug abuse violations;

     (C) making it a requirement that each employee to be engaged in the performance of such contract be given a copy of the statement required by subparagraph (A);

     (D) notifying the employee in the statement required by subparagraph (A), that as a condition of employment on such contract, the employee will

       (i) abide by the terms of the statement; and

       (ii) notify the employer of any criminal drug statute conviction for a violation occurring in the workplace no later than 5 days after such conviction;

     (E) notifying the contracting agency within 10 days after receiving notice under subparagraph (D)(ii) from an employee or otherwise receiving actual notice of such conviction;

(F)　imposing a sanction on, or requiring the satisfactory participation in a drug abuse assistance or rehabilitation program by, any employee who is so convicted, as required by section 5154; and

(G)　making a good faith effort to continue to maintain a drug-free workplace through implementation of subparagraphs (A), (B), (C), ((D), (E), and (F).

(2)　*Requirement for Individuals.* No Federal agency shall enter into a contract with an individual unless such contract includes a certification by the individual that the individual will not engage in the unlawful manufacture, distribution, dispensation, possession, or use of a controlled substance in the performance of the contract.

(b)　Suspension, Termination, or Debarment of the Contractor.

(1)　*Grounds for Suspension, Termination, or Debarment.* Each contract awarded by a Federal agency shall be subject to suspension of payments under the contract or termination of the contract, or both, and the contractor thereunder or the individual who entered the contract with the Federal agency, as applicable, shall be subject to suspension or debarment in accordance with the requirements of this section if the head of the agency determines that

(A)　the contractor or individual has made a false certification under subsection (a);

(B)　the contractor violates such certification by failing to carry out the requirements of subparagraph (A), (B), (C), (D), (E), or (F) of subsection (a)(1); or

(C)　such a number of employees of such contractor have been convicted of violations of criminal drug statutes for violations occurring in the workplace as to indicate that the contractor has failed to make a good faith effort to provide a drug-free workplace as required by subsection (a).

(2)　*Conduct of Suspension, Termination, and Debarment Proceedings.*

(A)　If a contracting officer determines, in writing, that cause for suspension of payments, termination, or suspension or debarment exists, an appropriate action shall be initiated by the contracting officer of the agency, to be conducted by the agency concerned in accordance with the Federal Acquisition Regulation and applicable agency procedures.

(B)　The Federal Acquisition Regulation shall be revised to include rules for conducting suspension and debarment proceedings under this subsection, including rules providing notice, opportunity to respond in writing or in person, and such other procedures as may be necessary to provide a full and fair proceeding to a contractor or individual in such proceeding.

(3)　*Effect of Debarment.* Upon issuance of any final decision under this subsection requiring debarment of a contractor or individual, such contractor or individual shall be ineligible for award of any contract by any Federal agency, and for participation in any future procurement by any Federal agency, for a period specified in the decision, not to exceed 5 years.

**Section 5153. Drug-Free Workplace Requirements for Federal Grant Recipients**

(a) Drug-Free Workplace Requirement.
  (1) *Persons Other Than Individuals.* No person, other than an individual, shall receive a grant from any Federal agency unless such person has certified to the granting agency that it will provide a drug-free workplace by
    (A) publishing a statement notifying employees that the unlawful manufacture, distribution, dispensation, possession, or use of a controlled substance is prohibited in the grantee's workplace and specifying the actions that will be taken against employees for violations of such prohibition;
    (B) establishing a drug-free awareness program to inform employees about
      (i) the dangers of drug abuse in the workplace;
      (ii) the grantee's policy of maintaining a drug-free workplace;
      (iii) any available drug counseling, rehabilitation, and employee assistance programs; and
      (iv) the penalties that may be imposed upon employees for drug abuse violations;
    (C) making it a requirement that each employee to be engaged in the performance of such grant be given a copy of the statement required by subparagraph (A);
    (D) notifying the employee in the statement required by subparagraph (A), that as a condition of employment on such grant, the employee will
      (i) abide by the terms of the statement; and
      (ii) notify the employer of any criminal drug statute conviction for a violation occurring in the workplace no later than 5 days after such conviction;
    (E) notifying the granting agency within 10 days after receiving notice under subparagraph (D)(ii) from an employee or otherwise receiving actual notice of such conviction;
    (F) imposing a sanction on, or requiring the satisfactory participation in a drug abuse assistance or rehabilitation program by, any employee who is so convicted, as required by section 5154; and
    (G) making a good faith effort to continue to maintain a drug-free workplace through implementation of subparagraphs (A), (B), (C), (D), (E), and (F).
  (2) *Individuals.* No Federal agency shall make a grant to any individual unless such individual certifies to the agency as a condition of such grant that the individual will not engage in the unlawful manufacture, distribution, dispensation, possession, or use of a controlled substance in conducting any activity with such grant.
(b) Suspension, Termination, or Debarment of the Grantee
  (1) *Grounds for Suspension, Termination, or Debarment.* Each grant awarded by a Federal agency shall be subject to suspension of payments under the grant or termination of the grant, or both, and the grantee thereunder shall be

subject to suspension or debarment in accordance with the requirements of this section if the agency of the granting agency determines, in writing, that

(A)  the grantee has made a false certification under subsection (a);

(B)  the grantee violates such certification by failing to carry out the requirements of subparagraph (A), (B), (C), (D), (E), or (F) or subsection (a)(1); or

(C)  such a number of employees of such grantee have been convicted of violations of criminal drug statutes for violations occurring in the workplace as to indicate that the grantee has failed to make a good faith effort to provide a drug-free workplace as required by subsection (a)(1).

(2)  *Conduct of Suspension, Termination, and Debarment Proceedings.* A suspension of payments, termination, or suspension or debarment proceeding subject to this subsection shall be conducted in accordance with applicable law, including Executive Order 12549 or any superseding Executive order and regulations promulgated to implement such law or Executive order.

(3)  *Effect of Debarment.* Upon issuance of any final decision under this subsection requiring debarment of any grantee, such grantee shall be ineligible for award of any grant by any Federal agency, and for participation in any future grant from any Federal agency for a period specified in the decision, not to exceed 5 years.

## Section 5154.  Employee Sanctions and Remedies

A grantee or contractor shall, within 30 days after receiving notice from an employee of a conviction pursuant to section 5152(a)(1)(D)(ii) or 5153(a)(1)(D)(ii),

(1)  take appropriate personnel action against such employee up to and including termination; or

(2)  require such employee to satisfactorily participate in a drug abuse assistance or rehabilitation program approved for such purposes by a Federal, State, or local health, law enforcement, or other appropriate agency.

## Section 51555.  Waiver

(a)  In general. A termination, suspension of payments, or suspension or debarment under this subtitle may be waived by the head of an agency with respect to a particular contract or grant if

(1)  in the case of a waiver with respect to a contract, the head of the agency determines under section 5152(b)(1), after the issuance of a final determination under such section, that suspension of payments, or termination of the contract, or suspension or debarment of the contractor, or refusal to permit a person to be treated as a responsible source for a contract, as the case may be, would severely disrupt the operation of such agency to the detriment of the Federal Government or the general public; or

(2)   in the case of a waiver with respect to a grant, the head of the agency determines that suspension of payments, termination of the grant, or suspension or debarment of the grantee would not be in the public interest.

(b)   Exclusive authority. The authority of the head of an agency under this section to waive a termination, suspension, or debarment shall not be delegated.

## Section 5156.  Regulations

Not later than 90 days after the date of enactment of this subtitle, the government-wide regulations governing actions under this subtitle shall be issued pursuant to the Office of Federal Procurement Policy Act (41 USC 401 et seq.).

## Section 5157.  Definitions

For the purposes of this subtitle

(1)   the term ''drug-free workplace'' means a site for the performance of work done in connection with a specific grant or contract described in section 5152 or 5153 or an entity at which employees of such entity are prohibited from engaging in the unlawful manufacture, distribution, dispensation, possession, or use of a controlled substance in accordance with the requirements of this Act.

(2)   the term ''employee'' means the employee of a grantee or contractor directly engaged in the performance of work pursuant to the provisions of the grant or contract described in section 5152 or 5153.

(3)   the term ''controlled substance'' means a controlled substance in schedules I through V of section 202 of the Controlled Substances Act (21 USC 812).

(4)   the term ''conviction'' means a finding of guilt (including a plea of nolo contendere) or imposition of sentence, or both, by any judicial body charged with the responsibility to determine violations of the Federal or State criminal drug statutes.

(5)   the term ''criminal drug statute'' means a criminal statute involving manufacture, distribution, dispensation, use, or possession of any controlled substance.

(6)   the term ''grantee'' means the department, division, or other unit of a person responsible for the performance under the grant.

(7)   the term ''contractor'' means the department, division, or other unit of a person responsible for the performance under the contract.

(8)   the term ''Federal agency'' means an agency as that term is defined in section 552(f) of title 5, United States Code.

## Section 5158.  Construction of Subtitle

Nothing in this subtitle shall be construed to require law enforcement agencies, if the head of the agency determines it would be inappropriate in connection with the agency's undercover operations, to comply with the provisions of this subtitle.

**Section 5159. Repeal of Limitation on Use of Funds**

Section 628 of Public Law 100-440 (relating to restrictions on the use of certain appropriated amounts) is amended

   (1)  by striking "(a)" after "Sec 628."; and
   (2)  by striking subsection (b).

**Section 5160. Effective Date**

Sections 5152 and 5153 shall be effective 120 days after the date of the enactment of this subtitle.

# Index

172    *Investigation of Substance Abuse in the Workplace*